Who says I'm OK? Really, who does? Here are a few choices. You decide.

—drugs
—the great American dream
—my family
—Eastern mysticism
—Transactional Analysis
—the Christian faith
—education
—the ultimate orgasm
—I say I'm OK!

In this book I have an option you can't refuse. Because you really are OK. In truth! Absolutely! Not partly, relatively, or tentatively. No fooling, no gimmicks. So read on, friend.

WHO SAYS I'M OK?

A CHRISTIAN USE OF TRANSACTIONAL ANALYSIS

ALAN REUTER Ph. D.

Publishing House
St. Louis   London

The author acknowledges with thanks the editorial assistance of William Buege in the revision and preparation of this book.

Concordia Publishing House, St. Louis, Missouri
Concordia Publishing House Ltd., London, E. C. 1
Copyright © 1974 Concordia Publishing House

MANUFACTURED IN THE UNITED STATES OF AMERICA

Library of Congress Cataloging in Publication Data

Reuter, Alan.
    Who says I'm O. K.?

    Includes bibliographical references.
      1. Christian life — 1960-   2. Transactional analysis. I. Title.
BV4501.2.R47   248'.4   74-13756
ISBN 0-570-03187-7

To Walter, friend and teacher, who first taught me to "rightly divide the word of truth," and especially for Patsy, with whom I have the joy of living out the Christian life-style.

CONTENTS

Preface

1. Christianity American Style   11

2. Christianity and TA in This Modern World   19

    Christianity for the 20th century   20
    The OK Psychology — Transactional Analysis   24

3. The Secular Experience of God   30

    Threat   30
    Self-justification   33
    Hurting others   36
    A Christian answer   38

4. What Is OKness, Really?   41

    TA vs. Christianity   41
    We need OKness   42
    Picking ourselves up   45
    Moralism — being good   47
    Misusing being good   49
    An answer   52

5. Of Course We're Guilty . . .   54

    Freud and TA   54
    What is guilt?   56
    The roots of guilt   59
    Anxiety   62
    The results of guilt   64

6. But Must We Remain Guilty?   69

    The treatment of guilt   69
    The TA myth   73
    Idols   76
    Freedom in spite of guilt   79

7. The Way We Are   84

    Society, civilization, and nature   85
    Threatened man   87
    The nature of the self   91

8. Christian, You're a New Man!   95

    The new self in action   95
    The baptismal life-style   99
    Example I: value-negating behavior   103
    Example II: a redeemed transaction   105

9. It's Up to You   109

Appendix   118

PREFACE

This book is about Christian faith and Transactional Analysis. Its general purpose is to let psychology illuminate your Christian self-understanding and to permit your Christian conviction to engage psychology in necessary dialog.

I'm OK, You're OK and *Games People Play*, two enormously popular books in recent years, encourage you to believe you're OK and, because you're OK, to feel worthy. Christianity believes you are OK because Christ has "worthed" you, has filled you with his worthiness.

Because of this considerable difference, it is certainly prudent for the somewhat confused and bewildered Christian to wonder how properly to respond to and use the "OKness psychology" explosion. How should we make use of the valid insights offered us by psychologists and still avoid that which is inimical to the Christian understanding of men and women as people standing under the judgment and grace of God?

My goal is to relate my faith to my experience by making the language and insights of Transactional Analysis available for the message of Christ to individual Christians and the church alike.

This book asks the basic question, How can I as Christian honestly use Transactional Analysis? Chapter 1 challenges the "I as Christian" part of that statement. Chapter 2 introduces real Christianity and Transactional Analysis as live options in our world. Chapter 3 suggests that both real Christianity and TA attack the crucial problem of the threatened life. Chapter 4 indicates that for the real Christian, TA's answer to threat is superficial. Chapter 5 presents guilt as the result of threatened lives. Chapter 6 addresses two responses to guilt — TA's easy OK and Christianity's absolute OK. Chapters 7 and 8 propose an honest way for the real Christian to make TA a part of his new life in Christ. Finally, in chapter 9 you can see that this book is up to you.

The argument of my book is carefully developed and challenges you as an adult Christian. It comprises the body of the text and addresses the Adult in you.

I have also inserted special "appeal" sections because I would like all of each of you to respond to this book. Some are short stories, some are questions, puzzles, challenges, poems, and songs. Some are very serious. Some are just fun. They invite the Child and the Parent in you to participate.

Throughout this book study these new understandings. Work with them, discuss them, *argue with them*, participate in them. Perhaps you may want to keep a pen handy to cross out out or mark up particularly aggressive statements. In the end I hope the thrilling "ah ha!" experience of discovery will reward your effort as it has mine.

ALAN REUTER

CHRISTIANITY
AMERICAN STYLE

We live
in a culture in which Sunday morning is set aside for those
who want to pursue the "hobby" of religion. They can get
together and talk about God, faith, church budgets, con-
gregational dinners, getting to heaven, and the like, while
others are free to pursue their hobbies, such as golf, tennis,
or cutting grass. It is clear that religion in our culture has
become compartmentalized. It is an entirely optional,
leisure-time activity.

When asked about the role of religion in his life, an
executive of the Ford Motor Company candidly replied
that his faith had nothing to do with any of his business
decisions, practices, or general day-to-day living. It in no
way influenced him other than to encourage his effort to
be a "nice guy" and to try to do reasonably good things so
that God would be pleased with him. Indeed, he saw no
other way that he could relate religion to his life.

How about you?

Is it possible that we Christians have been leading secular lives not only outside of the church, but also within it,
where we least expect to find secularity? Secularism is

more than just antagonism or indifference toward religion; it is the loss of the relationship between religion and reality. Secularism means that religion is not a meaningful way for us to look at and interpret our lives. Secularism is not primarily doubt in God, faith, or salvation, but the inability to understand what such words mean, what they are saying to us, and how they are related to the way we experience reality as we encounter it in daily living.

The problem secularism (loss of the relationship between religion and experienced reality) forces on us is how intelligibly to relate these two "worlds" to each other and to ourselves. Solving this problem by carefully explaining everything that is said and done, as is being attempted in some churches, turns Christianity primarily into an educational enterprise, and faith into information. This is arid intellectualism. There is also no assurance that explaining what words, concepts, and actions mean will in turn relate them meaningfully to *our* experience. Anyone who has sat through endless esoteric Bible classes knows this painfully well. This is the danger of meaninglessness.

How do you cope with meaninglessness?

Imagine you are a member of a church evangelism team in Los Angeles. A young couple are explaining to you with great sadness that they have not rejected the church, but that they just don't bother to go anymore because it just doesn't make sense to them anymore, nor is it any help to them as they face their problem areas of life.

How do you answer this couple? What can you say to them? If you were the couple, what would you want to hear? A parental response:

"You *ought* to be in church"? Or a child response: "Naughty, naughty, aren't you terrible!" Or an adult consideration of their problem?

Now imagine it is a sunny Sunday morning in midsummer and you are in a Lutheran church in the small fishing town of Lemvig, Denmark. All is well. Or is it? Look around. Where is everyone? Why are there only white-haired old people? Why no youth or families?

Try to get the feeling of the situation. How does the church smell? Is the air warm or cool? Are you tense? How does your lower back feel against the pew? What will you do after the service?

Now, carefully, what are you thinking? Why?

Moralism, as well as intellectualism, also results from an unsuccessful attempt to bridge the gulf between religion and experience and reduces Christianity to moral admonition. "Be a nice guy because Jesus was!" "The good Samaritan helped others and so should you!" These moral lessons drawn from Scripture at least make an attempt to show how Christianity is related to life and experience. We all experience occasions when we could be better and help others more. But in the process they reduce Christianity to a series of ethical obligations. And faith once again loses its unique redemptive meaning, which itself needs to be experienced.

Why does moralism cause faith to lose its unique redemptive meaning?
Say "The good Samaritan helped others and

so should you" several times. Let it run through your mind. Whose voice do you hear speaking these words? Your old Sunday school teacher's? Your mother's?

Now make up some other sentences like that. "(The) _____ (did) _____ and so should you." Imagine you are saying them to someone. To whom? Imagine someone is saying them to you. How do you feel? Where are you? What are you wearing? What has happened to your adult faith? Does it continue to have the same meaning?

Christianity must be in the meaning business. It must spell out a meaning for life which a man can understand and by which he can interpret his life experiences. The problem is that Christianity is not the only game in town. It is in competition. There are countless other options around, all vying for our acceptance of them as our most important value in life, our highest meaning to which all other meanings are subservient. They range from the ridiculous, "Buick, something to believe in," to the more sophisticated — socialism, family, work, pleasure, power, prestige, or patriotism. Many of these are good in and of themselves, but none can occupy the position of highest meaning in our life without related consequences.

The man who makes his country his highest value has that kind of "my country right or wrong" patriotism that justifies whatever is done, and is actually a disservice to his country, which needs the moral guidance of its people.

Christianity must face it: these options which call for full, unlimited, and unquestioning acceptance are all pervasive. We Christians must make clear that our faith-life is a meaningful, nondestructive alternative to secularism, offering a unique, redemptive option which is *the only real alternative*. We must build new foundations.

The task of doing foundational theology is to see in what way we can reconnect experience and the Gospel. That is fundamental.

At this point many would object. Christianity has the answers. The task is simply to proclaim them. The task of the hearer is to accept them. But this is ignoring the situation the church finds itself in today. It is no longer possible to appeal to the traditional authorities. Outside of a church context it would be almost impossible to win any argument by appealing to the Pope or the Bible for support. We no longer have the power to impose external standards of proof on individuals. Many people will no longer accept statements because "the Bible tells me so" or because the President, Prime Minister, Pope, or clergyman says it, but only if it "grabs them where they're at." We cannot "prove" the truth claims of the Gospel from without. Its trustworthiness must be experienced from within. The Reformation already anticipated just such a situation when it rejected the external authority of popes and councils for the internal authority of the experience of the Gospel itself as proclaimed by Scripture.

It is, of course, possible to go on as we have been, as though there were no problem and as though secularism were something that exists only outside the church. But then we risk the meaninglessness that results when answers are given in the church that are not grounded in commonly experienced "question" situations of life. The phrase "God is the answer!" often appears on signs and billboards. One is tempted to respond, "What was the question?" The sign "Jesus saves" evokes similar questions,

"From what?" or "For what?"

Despite the obvious piety of such answers, the questions are equally important. Or to put it another way, the answer without the question is meaningless. Heinz Zahrnt accuses the church of being an "answering church," which often gives answers to questions that are not even being asked. Instead he would call the church to be a questioning church, whose concern it is to seek to ask the right questions.[1] This is really to ask Christian theology to attend to its foundations in life.

When a building is sinking, it is a good idea to check the foundation rather than the roof. The task of doing foundational theology is to see in what way we can reconnect experience and the Gospel.

This book is about you and theology and psychology. Psychology is the discipline that concerns itself with the self, how it perceives, is shaped, functions, feels emotion, and responds to experiences. If we discover that "you" are the common ground where theology and psychology come together, then we can begin to reground our theology in experience and begin to perceive that experience is not another word for secular and that we 20th-century Christians need not be people divided against ourselves. We can face the crisis facing the church. "What the Reformation proclaimed as Gospel can be heard in the lived experience of man's life today."[2]

For each item circle the answer that more nearly applies to you. Then cross out the answer you think is the more secular one.

[1] *What Kind of God?* (Minneapolis: Augsburg Publishing House, 1972), pp. 69—88.

[2] Wenzel Lahff, "Justification and Anthropology," *CTM*. XLIV, 1 (January 1973), 33.

1. (A) Do you see the Christian faith as primarily concerned with your everyday life, or (B) with a way of gaining heaven and eternal life?

2. (A) Should your pastor preach on such things as war, racial prejudice, sex, and politics, or (B) should he limit himself to religious matters?

3. (A) Are the things you do in church typical of things you do everyday, or (B) are they different?

4. (A) Are the hymns you sing intelligible and meaningful for you, or (B) do they seem to come from another time and place, with thoughts and language you would not normally use?

5. (A) Should your pastor or denomination criticize our country and culture, or (B) is the church's role to reinforce and support what our country and government do?

6. (A) Are there any situations in your everyday life, apart from church, where you use words like *redemption, justification, sanctification, God, angels, devil, heaven,* or (B) usually aren't there?

7. (A) Do you find concepts such as the Trinity helpful to you in understanding the Christian faith, or (B) are they "divine mysteries" we should accept?

8. (A) Would you attend a church where the things you value were criticized, or (B) would you prefer a church that stands for the things you believe in?

9. Is it more important to (A) support local welfare projects, like day-care centers, run by your church or denomination or (B) give money to build a new church building?

10. (A) Is it possible for someone to be a good doctor and not believe in or pray to God, or (B) usually isn't it?

11. (A) Does your belief in God affect you in a way that

pleases you in your day-to-day decisions, or (B) doesn't it?

12. (A) Do your Bibles and your pastor's sermons have more influence on your life, or (B) do TV shows, commercials, magazines, and novels?

13. (B) Does the passage in the Bible that says we should be in the world but not of it show us that spiritual concerns and earthly concerns must be separated, or (A) doesn't it?

Now you can compare your answers with the answers of others.

Most people feel that for all the questions *B* better reflects their beliefs and actions. In other words, most of us have experienced "the loss of relation between religion and reality." By our earlier definition we have become secular.

Most people feel that where the question is applicable, answer *A* was the more secular answer. For example, in relation to question four, many feel that putting hymns in today's language or using "modern" hymns to replace old favorites is secular.

Our answers often reveal just how much we have viewed the church as separate from life, as a compartment with no relationship to our real concerns. Some sort of healing of this polarization will be necessary for religion to become an integral and vital part of our lives and society.

2.
CHRISTIANITY AND TA IN THIS MODERN WORLD

Suppose you went to a pastor for counseling? What would you expect of him? Would you expect him to talk about God and faith, or would you expect him to use the most appropriate psychological technique available?

Just such a problem causes great frustration among seminarians and pastors when they try to function as psychologists after one or two required courses in pastoral psychology. Is more training the answer, or does the problem lie elsewhere? Does saying a prayer at the end of a Rogerian therapy session make it "Christian" counseling? In an age weaned on Freud what is the fate of the traditional view of pastoral ministry as the care of souls? Perhaps all pastors should turn over their shepherds' crooks to the neighborhood psychiatrist, who is after all better trained than they could ever hope to be.

One minister recently commented:

> For the past 16 years this writer has had the mistaken notion that if he could do good, competent, secular psychotherapy in a church building or while wearing a clerical collar, somehow it would come out as pastoral

care. He sensed that this notion is as unsatisfactory for many of his colleagues as it is for himself.[3]

Many critiques of religion have been done from the viewpoint of psychology, but little has been done to test the adequacy of psychological theories and therapeutic techniques in the light of theology to see whether they form an adequate base from which to meaningfully view the Gospel. This chapter prepares for such a test by clarifying, What is Christianity? and, What is TA?

Christianity for the 20th century

Theology today is the systematic effort to understand the meaning and implications of the experience of God and of the faith it produces. The Biblical experience of God is always either of His judgment or His grace, His threat or His affirmation.

In Old Testament times God was threateningly experienced as Judge in such everyday occurrences as sickness, death, persecution, enslavement, defeat at the hands of enemies, and as Rescuer from that judgment. The central event of rescue around which the whole Old Testament revolves is the event of the Exodus. So great, in fact, was this event and so decisive for Israel's life as a people that later experiences of rescue were interpreted in its light. This experience of God's judgment and grace was then described in terms of everyday events. God became Shepherd, Father, the Judge, and the Avenging Relative, who makes things right on our behalf.

To say God is our Father or the Good Shepherd is to use a model from human experience by which we under-

---

[3] David Belgum, *Guilt: Where Psychology and Religion Meet* (Englewood Cliffs: Prentice Hall, Inc., 1963), p. 3.

stand what God means to us. A model is an image which suggests the structure of whatever it refers to.

> The models or metaphors we use to help us understand God usually reflect our own world. Let your imagination free for a minute. Construct a minitheology for each of the following persons, a theology where the terms and concepts are borrowed from their own life experiences:
> 1. An eskimo
> 2. A pigmy living the rain forests of Africa
> 3. A mountain man in the American Rockies, 1845
> 4. A spacewoman from the U.S.A. living on Mars in 2121
> 5. An American suburbanite in the 1970s

The model of God as a supernatural, personal being became the primary one in the Middle Ages. But it also became increasingly separated from the primary experiences of God in life as judgment, threat, and affirmation. This medieval model has been equal to the total reality of God for men and human experience for a long time. But it is not where our primary experience of the reality is!

For many the model has become so separated from its grounding in life and common experience that it has been trivialized (God is a nice old man in the sky with a long white beard, who overlooks the foolish foibles of his errant children) or denied (there is no such supernatural world and being).

Here is a picture of God. Does it adequately reflect your 20th-century experience of reality? How? How not?

Imagine creating your own visual model of God. What kind of photograph or painting do you perceive? Why?

But our experience of God is of judgment and grace, threat and rescue from that threat, the experience of being called into question and saved by the Questioner.

We may have to do theology today in a new way, a way that shows the experience of God in our culture not as the experience of the supernatural but initially as the experience of threat and judgment. If we tie the Christian proclamation to a cultural spirit and self-understanding no longer held by most (that is, tie it to a medieval understanding), then we place ourselves at a disadvantage in our culture and risk missing the point of the Christian proclamation.

Our message is not that the supernatural exists and that we must believe that, but rather that in the midst of threat there is an affirming event that has taken place in Jesus of Nazareth. The Christian faith offers this redemptive alternative to the self-made, deceptive, and illusory affirmations that men trust in the face of threat. The question is whether a man trust in ultimate threat or in ultimate affirmation, and not whether or not the supernatural exists.

This is a picture like those sometimes used in psychological testing. Look it over, and in a relaxed fashion (don't edit all your ideas) tell yourself a story about the picture (time, place, events leading up to the picture, away from it, participants, and especially the emotion in the picture).

Now examine your story. Is it basically a threatening or an affirming story? Can you pin the details to events in your own life? Do you feel that you often threaten others? Is the experience of God for you in your world a positive one, or would you rather not have Him around?

If secularism is the spirit of our times, then the Gospel will be relevant only if it resists total capitulation to this secular spirit (total absorption in social action, civil rights, or revolution) and at the same time uses categories, models, and metaphors familiar to contemporary life and thought. This can be done by placing the religious dimension of life into the realm of experienced threat and affirmation, values, value choices, meaning, and OKness and not-OKness.

We can only speak of God as He has dealt with us and as we experience His verdict on us, whether threateningly in our life and history or redemptively in the life and history of Jesus, our liberator.

Although the "from what" and the "for what" of that liberation have changed, the church has always confessed that Jesus is the Liberator. How people experience Jesus today and the psychological categories appropriate to describing that liberation are major concerns for us as we encounter Transactional Analysis.

The OK psychology — Transactional Analysis

Transactional analysis was popularized and gained widespread influence through the work of Eric Berne and Thomas Harris. It is being taught and used in hundreds of centers throughout the country with great enthusiasm and in many seminaries of all denominations. (This, of course, also highlights the problem of how one functions in Christian counseling with a supposedly secular technique. Is the only concern whether or not Transactional Analysis is effective?) Once again the question arises: Does a pastor's use of Transactional Analysis make it "Christian" counseling?

Thomas Oden's caustic comments about the "encounter culture" seem to be applicable to the growth and spread of Transactional Analysis:

> Its apostolic tradition is handed down from the 'saints' [Berne, Harris], fervently believed by those who are susceptible to belief, and enthusiastically propagated by missionaries committed to the evangelization of the world in this generation.[4]

Many other activities have "apostolic traditions," "saints," fervent believers, and missionaries: political theories obviously, sports activities like baseball, and life styles.

List some you can think of that you are involved in. Decide who are the saints, what is the apostolic tradition, etc. For the individual items, where do you see yourself? Are you a missionary of Suburban Life, a fervent believer in Tennis?

What significance do these secular religions have for you as Christian?

Our question must be whether Transactional Analysis has an understanding of man that is capable of providing an adequate basis for the proclamation of the Gospel. Remember, TA is both a counseling technique *and* a current model for understanding man — a model that must be examined to see if it is compatible with the Christian understanding of man.

Transactional Analysis uses individual responses, called transactions, as its unit of analysis.[5] People respond

[4] *The Intensive Group Experience* (Philadelphia: The Westminster Press, 1972), p. 89.

[5] The following is a summary of material found in Thomas Harris, *I'm OK — You're OK: A Practical Guide to Transactional Analysis* (New

to each other in any of three ways corresponding to three ego states that exist in all people. These are a Parent, an Adult, and a Child (P-A-C). *Parent, Adult,* and *Child* are capitalized in Transactional Analysis to show the special usage and meaning given these terms.

The Parent (P) is made up of attitudes received as a child primarily of a controlling, manipulative nature, and also of a nurturing nature. Recent brain research has shown that all of a person's experiences from birth, and possibly before birth, are recorded by the brain much like a tape recording. The Parental tape records, along with all other experiences, the thousands of negative "don'ts" and "no-no's" without realizing the preservational intention of most of these injunctions. Together with the experience, the emotions felt at the time are also recorded.

The Adult (A) ego state is a mature, responsible response pattern concerned with decision making, value judgments, and future planning.

The Child (C) is a dependent, immature response, often self-centered and self-seeking, reflecting basic drives and instincts. It is also the source of energy, creativity, and spontaneity.

Transactional Analysis uses diagrams to illustrate the transaction which is taking place. For example, an Adult-to-Adult transaction would be diagrammed as in A-A below (Fig. 1). A Parent-Child transaction would be as in Figure 2. Basic complementary transactions are P-P, A-A, and C-C.

Such transactions as P-C are also complementary if both persons want to remain in their respective ego state. This occurs in some marriages where one partner acts predominantly from a Parent ego state and the other from

York: Harper and Row, 1967), pp. 1–96; and Eric Berne, *Games People Play* (New York: Grove Press, Inc., 1964), pp. 1–34.

the Child ego state, and both are willing to continue in this manner. If one person makes a P-C transaction and the other responds with an A-A transaction, the lines cross, and this indicates a disruptive situation (Fig. 3).

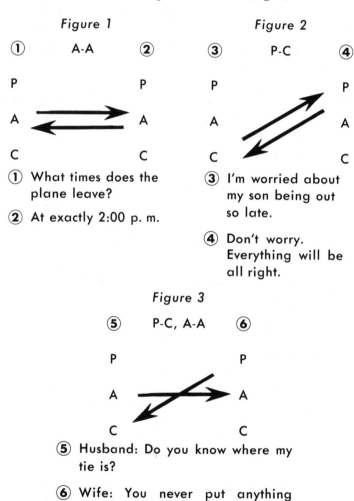

Figure 1

①   A-A   ②

P   P

A   A

C   C

① What times does the plane leave?

② At exactly 2:00 p. m.

Figure 2

③   P-C   ④

P   P

A   A

C   C

③ I'm worried about my son being out so late.

④ Don't worry. Everything will be all right.

Figure 3

⑤   P-C, A-A   ⑥

P   P

A   A

C   C

⑤ Husband: Do you know where my tie is?

⑥ Wife: You never put anything away!

The goal of Transactional Analysis is to sensitize people into an awareness of which ego state they are expressing and the position into which it puts others. By moving from disruptive to complementary transactions, a person can develop more satisfying interpersonal relationships. The ideal transaction is the Adult-Adult transaction. Here the mature, rational Adult is in control, and one is in the realm of open and satisfying exchange.

This, of course, is only the most rudimentary explication of Transactional Analysis. Readers are referred to the basic works on Transactional Analysis for a full presentation. Perhaps the clearest, most concise, and well organized presentation is *Born to Win*.

Born to Win [6] uses psychological exercises to help you achieve the more satisfying interpersonal relationships it discusses. Here are three quoted examples. If you find them interesting, you may want to purchase the book.

You and Touch

To become more aware of your touch patterns, reflect on the last 48 hours. Evaluate your capacity to give and receive touch.
- Whom did you touch? How did you touch them? Positively? Negatively?
- Did you avoid touching someone? Why? Do you wish you had touched someone? Why?
- Who touched you? How did they touch you? Positively? Negatively?

[6] Muriel James and Dorothy Jongeward, *Born to Win: Transactional Analysis with Gestalt Experiments* (Reading, Mass.: Addison-Wesley Publishing Co., 1971). Reprinted by permission.

- Did you avoid letting someone touch you? Why? Do you wish someone had touched you?
  — p. 64

On Stage

Imagine your life drama being performed on a stage.

- Is it a comedy, a farce, a saga, a soap opera, a melodrama, a tragedy, or what?
- Does your play have a script theme? If so, is it success-oriented or failure-oriented — constructive, destructive, or nonproductive?
- Be the audience watching your play. Do you applaud, cry, boo, laugh, go to sleep, want your money back, or what?
  — p. 99

This fantasy experiment is for those who have forgotten, are afraid, or feel unable to play. Do the experiments gradually. Stop if you become too anxious. Wait a while and start again. Don't rush yourself.

- Imagine yourself getting ready to play a game of volleyball.
- Select what to wear. Visualize yourself dressed and ready to play.
- Imagine yourself on the way to the game.
- See yourself and others arriving at the court.
- Visualize yourself on the court hitting some good shots and missing others.
- Let your excitement flow freely. See yourself smiling, laughing, yelling, running, leaping, scooping up the ball, having fun.
  — p. 183

3.
THE SECULAR EXPERIENCE OF GOD

Both Christianity and TA address themselves to what it means to live under threat, to feeling not-OK, and to how we can get out from under threat and feel truly OK.

Threat

Man regularly experiences threat. The word *threat* is used throughout this book as a kind of shorthand symbol for a whole "structure of existence" under which we live. In the face of threat he asks himself, "How can I survive? Why do bad things happen to me? Why shouldn't I pass those bad things on to others?"

Threat attacks man's meaning in life. And life's meaning is tested by how well it can bear up under threat. Do our ultimate meanings, our gods, sustain us in times of threat, or do they fail? Or is unconditional threat itself an experience of God?

Langdon Gilkey does an extensive analysis of the secular experience of God and concludes that it is not in fact the experience of a supreme person or a supernatural being, but the experience of threat.[7] God is experienced as a threatening void, as an absence rather than a presence. It is the experience of a threatening void that sends men fleeing to fill it. It is an absence not only of the existence of God, but of ultimate love and ultimate affirmation, the absence of the triumph of life, reason, order, and meaning.

This is a very short story by the former Beatle John Lennon. It is a story of threat and destruction at a time of peace, Christmas. Notice that the language is also threatened and partly destroyed in the story. You as reader are being threatened too. Imagine for a moment that there really is no redeeming God, only all-powerful threat. Then let this story settle on your mind — both the content and the attack on language. Do you feel now how your secular neighbor may feel?

Randolf's Party

It was Chrisbus time but Randolph was alone. Where were all his good pals. Bernie, Dave, Nicky, Alice, Beddy, Freba, Viggy, Nigel, Alfred, Clive, Stan, Frenk, Tom, Harry, George, Harold? Where were they on this day? Randolf looged saggly at his only Chrispbut cart from his dad who did not live there.

"I can't understan this being so aloneley on the one day of the year when one would surely spect a pal or two?" thought Rangolf. Hanyway he carried on putting ub the desicrations and muzzle toe. All of a surgeon

[7] Langdon Gilkey, *Naming the Whirlwind: The Renewal of God Language* (Indianapolis: The Bobbs-Merrill Co., 1969), part II, chapters 3 and 4. See also Helmut Thielicke, *Death and Life* (Philadelphia: Fortress Press, 1970), pp. 105 ff.

there was amerry timble on the door. Who but who could be a knocking on my door? He opened it and there standing there who? but only his pals. Bernie, Dave, Nicky, Alice, Beddy, Freba, Viggy, Nigel, Alfred, Clive, Stan, Frenk, Tom, Harry, George, Harolb weren't they?

Come on in old pals buddys and mates. With a big griff on his face Randoff welcombed them. In they came jorking and labbing shoubing "Haddy Grimmble, Randoob." and other hearty, and then they all jumbed on him and did smite him with mighty blows about his head crying, "We never liked you all the years we've known you. You were never really one of us you know, soft head."

They killed him you know, at least he didn't die alone did he? Merry Chrustchove, Raldolf old pal buddy.[8]

Gilkey lists four characteristics of the secular spirit:
1. *contingency* — The world is not dependent on anything.
2. *relativity* — There are no absolutes. Everything must be seen from the point of view of the individual observer.
3. *transcience* — Nothing is forever. This is all we've got. Or as the beer commercial says, "You only go around once!"
4. *autonomy* — Man is on his own. It's up to him to shape his environment and create for himself whatever meaning there is.

These characteristics seem initially to be liberating and freeing. They seem to be the expression of the mature adult where man has finally come of age and is no longer childishly dependent or controlled from outside himself.

[8] John Lennon, *In His Own Write* (New York: Simon & Schuster, Inc., 1964). Reprinted by permission.

They are, however, actually perceived as threatening. For if the world is not dependent on anything, then it is neither necessary, purposive, nor rational. There is no meaning. Life is only the result of blind forces, chemicals accidently coming together in the vast recesses of space. Everything is relative. There are no authorities, no absolutes. Whatever meaning there is, man must create for himself in the brief time he exists.

This is the threatening void left by the absence of God. This threat to existence is experienced ultimately in death, which reduces all that we are, have been, and hope to be, to nothing, to a zero, to cosmic dust forever floating in infinity. Death says "No" to us in an ultimate, inescapable way. And no matter how hard we "grab for gusto" we realize that finally, in the last analysis, we are truly not-OK. We are not affirmed. We are not vindicated.

This ultimate threat is mediated to us through hundreds of relative daily threatening experiences beginning at birth and in childhood, which we perceive as threatening and which, as Transactional Analysis affirms, tell us we are not-OK.

Threat as an experience of God is shown vividly in the words of a woman who has not experienced love of any kind in her life. She said to the pastor who visited her in a mental institution, "I don't care if God cares — do you?"

What would you say to her? How could you answer?

Self-justification

The problem is compounded by the obligation we feel upon ourselves to be OK. There is an *oughtness* hanging over our existence. We feel accountable and responsible, and we feel the compulsion to justify not only our actions and activities but the whole of our existence. So we search for some meaning to defend ourselves and give god-like allegiance to, and cling to whatever meaning, person, or thing affirms us.

As we experience ultimate threat in our struggle with guilt, anxiety, and meaningless emptiness, we seek to find something or someone to justify ourselves, to give us meaning, and so we elevate limited values and relative good to the level of ultimate sources of meaning and value.

Even the suicide, who takes threat with absolute seriousness, seeks to justify his existence from beyond the grave when he leaves behind a note explaining what drove him to do what he has done. Even pity is preferable to the absence of affirmation.

Laurence Olivier revealed how this worked in himself in a recent interview. His parents were poor, and he experienced threat both in the negations of his life by an authoritative, judgmental father, who had not wanted another mouth to feed, and by the death of his mother when he was 12. She had been the only one to give him any kind of affirmation, and he was totally dependent on her so that her passing shattered his world. These scars and the threatening not-OKness of his childhood left him with a deep self-hatred which exists to this day. His only release is his acting, where he can become another character, another person, and for that time feel OK. His acting is the only meaning, the only affirmation of his life. And so he lives other people's lives in a dream world of illusion by which he affirms himself and escapes the threatening, destructive self-hatred of reality.

The tragedy of our gods is that they do not justify us

in the final analysis. They fail us, and we mourn their passing. Threat becomes more potent as our defenses fail to defend and we are faced with judgment for our idolatries, our bad faith, and our misplaced trust.

Joan Baez' very popular song "Blessed Are" is a powerful explication of the human situation. It has been especially popular with young people.

Get a copy of the song. Listen to it, then read it. Imagine you are a 20-year-old young man or lady in the late sixties. You have long hair, wear faded jeans, feel like dropping out of college, are involved in the Viet Nam war, and are sitting on a rainy beach in Northern California, with heavy traffic noise in the background. Try to express your feelings toward the song. How do they differ from the way you would react as yourself?

After doing that, read it again imagining you are a parent, and the person I've just described above and you've just imagined yourself to be is your child. What would you say to him or her? Change roles and answer yourself from the child's point of view.

It is clear, however, that we do not experience living in the "shadow of God" in pain, retribution, weeping, tears, death, and suicide as blessing, but rather as damnation. And the hope offered us in our own limited joy and submissive pacification rings hollow, unsatisfactory, illusory, and impotently ineffective in rescuing us from such hell.

Hurting others

Not only are our response to threat and the illusions we live by self-damaging, they are also damaging to others as we pass on the hurt and exploit others to build ourselves up in an ever widening *cycle of retribution.*

Genesis 3 describes this cycle of retribution which results from our attempts at self-justification. Adam and Eve ˗ are engaged in self-justification. Eve says, "The serpent tempted me," and Adam responds, "The woman tempted me," as they both seek to avoid responsibility and complicity. They offer excuses and thus become the legitimizers of their own existence. The result is expulsion from the garden, an end of innocence, and the possibility for death. Death always ends self-justification by showing our failure to legitimize and secure our existence from threat.

Furthermore, not only do we blame each other, but all attempts at self-justification are an implicit blaming of God. Adam says, "The woman *You* gave me." I am not guilty because of the world *You* made, the circumstances *You* give me to live under. We would all like to see ourselves as innocent victims, but threat and death keep haunting us and often push past our defenses to reveal our guilt, complicity, and accountability.

We try as much as possible to avoid the truth about ourselves and to retreat from encounter with God as Adam did in his blaming of Eve. In George Orwell's *1984*, as a rat cage is about to be lowered over a man's head, he says, "Do it to the woman" (the woman he has dearly loved). We all say similar things: "Do it to the black. Do it to the Jew. Do it to anyone but me!" In this manner we get false affirmations from our race, our whiteness (or blackness), from our continual need to insist that we are always right.

36

Others as well as ourselves must pay the price. For self-justification is always done at the expense of others and of the truth, and the cost is dear. Husband blames wife; wife blames husband. Nation blames nation. Political parties accuse each other. Rightwingers blame radical "pinkos," and "rad-libs" blame the "establishment straights." Women blame men, while men humor or exploit women.

Hurt is unavoidable as we limit the possibilities of our fellow men to serve our own needs, and as we blame each other we blame God. We didn't ask to be born. It's not our fault! A woman whose marriage had failed (largely her own fault, but she blamed "that miserable rat") profoundly concluded that "life is a cheat," meaning it was God's fault not hers. Life (read "God") owed her something. Then she met a wonderful man (got affirmation) and concluded, "Life isn't a cheat after all!"

We all have a pantheon of values, and crisis situations determine which of them we elevate to positions of ultimacy. Look at the kinds of value choices we make. The Watergate participants were willing to sacrifice honesty, truth, law, and morality for victory and loyalty to one man. The consequences were that anyone who disagreed was "the enemy" to be beaten no matter what rights were ignored in this war mentality.

B. F. Skinner, the noted behavioral psychologist, said in all seriousness on a television talk show that if forced to choose between burning his books and burning his children, he would burn his children. This reveals the depths to which we will go in order to preserve our affirmations.

One way to discover the reality of threat is to let your image-creating self free-associate things and situations to the experience of threat. Below

is the result of one person's efforts and his subsequent interpretation. Try the same exercise yourself.

> Approached by the tiger, the bear,
> the white-haired old man with his knife,
> I step back.
>
> The tiger crouches
> and I step back.
> The bear growls.
> Back over the curb.
> The man laughs silently, raises his knife.
> Back to the wall.
>
> Wordsworth knew it well.
> Childhood is best
> and life is in embryo.
>
> I am up against the wall
> and they are laughing.

"Because we are always under the ultimate threat of death, we constantly attack others and are ourselves attacked. We tend to scurry away from death, retreating back into childish responses, back to infancy. There we discover the blank wall of birth on one side, the dark wall of old age and death closing in from the other. And we are alone."

A Christian answer

We have said that the contemporary experience of God is one of ultimate threat. If there is any rescue, it is not in the elevation of relative values but in another ultimate verdict. The assertion of the Christian community is that of the surprise of the Gospel. Miracle of miracles! The thing we least expected or could not even dare hope for has happened: God our enemy, the slayer of our gods, our justifiable accuser, has become our Friend, our Vindicator, our Affirmer!

We know that threat is grounded in our personal experience and history. The ultimate affirmation of God is also grounded in history, in the historical event of Jesus of Nazareth, who comes to us as God the Affirmer. When we trust in that affirmation, His history becomes our history, and God's affirmation is experienced in our personal history as freedom from despair and from the need for false gods and self-contrived illusory affirmations.

The Christian faith results in a shifting of values and the continual struggle to trust the Affirmer with ultimate seriousness rather than the Accuser, whom we also continue to experience. It is the faith which trusts the love of God in spite of and in the face of this continuing threat.

This puts the Christian faith in its most uncomfortable but clearest focus. It means, for example, that when death occurs we don't "comfort" the relatives with saccharine sentimentalities that deny the existence of threat and the awesome reality of death: "It's all part of God's great plan," or "God must have a reason for calling Jimmy home. It's all for the best." Rather such occasions call for the proclamation of the love of God in spite of and in the face of the very real fact of death or illness. The occasion calls for gently calling all to trust in God's love and not the threatening negation happening in death or illness.

Jesus tells a paralytic that his sins are forgiven, meaning he is free to trust Jesus' affirming word and not what is happening to him in his paralysis. Occasions of crisis call for trust in God's love and not some kind of fatalistic submission to an abstract "divine will," which is really only the acknowledgement of the inevitability of threat. To do less than to present the Christian faith in its sharpest focus as such an alternative is to sacrifice the truth and live in illusion about the true reality and radical contingencies of the human situation.

OK_{NESS,} 4. WHAT IS REALLY?

What place is there for Transactional Analysis in pastoral counseling? Should it be used exclusively, in a supplementary manner, or not at all? How should individual Christians properly use it?

TA vs. Christianity

First of all it must be clear that while the goals of Transactional Analysis and the Christian faith are not inimical, they are also not identical. Christianity asserts that the human situation is the result of a broken relationship with God. Man's alienation from God is reflected in his relationship to himself, to his fellow men, and to his world. Thus sin spreads like ripples around a rock thrown in still water, to disturb all the dimensions of life.

Transactional Analysis states that the basic posture of man is the not-OK feeling. This is a statement based on empirical analysis of the nature of birth and childhood. A person feels not-OK in his relationships, initially with his parents, then with others (man-to-man). Christianity asserts that there is also a cosmic or ultimate dimension

41

of not-OKness. Not only do others tell me that I'm not-OK, but all the reality of my being in the world, ending in death, confers and confirms on me an unconditional not-OKness, an unconditional threat, which is itself an experience of God (man-to-God), albeit a negative one.

Transactional Analysis deals with the self in order to facilitate good relationships between persons. Thus it does not deal consciously, nor explicitly, with what Christianity feels is the "gut issue," the theological issue, man's primary relationship to God.

It may seem unfair to accuse Transactional Analysis of leaving out the God relationship since one could hardly expect otherwise from a secular therapy. But as we shall see, Transactional Analysis does in fact deal with the God dimension in an unconscious, but implicit, manner as it views man. If there is validity to the claims of the Christian faith about the primacy of the God relation, then it is ultimately impossible to separate the God relation from the other relationships a man has.

Finally, Transactional Analysis treats religion only tangentially and not as the basic issue of human life. It views Christianity largely as one source of values rather than the questioner of values.

But religion is something all men have, and faith is common to all, not only the experience of a few. Christianity is concerned with *what* a man trusts. It is not a question of whether or not there is faith, but faith in what. TA also must concern itself with the fact that mankind is a faith-full people.

We need OKness

We have seen that the contemporary experience of God is the experience of threat and also the experience of ultimate affirmation for those who put their trust in Jesus the affirmer.

It is now possible to relate this to Transactional Analysis' understanding of man. Transactional Analysis views man as in need of OKness. Man is obligated to believe he is accepted, affirmed, OK. However Transactional Analysis never explains why we should believe we are OK. It only affirms that we want to feel OK because the not-OK feeling is so severe, debilitating, and destructive in its consequences to our lives.

Try to remember several times recently when you have been complimented. After detailing each experience in your mind, say aloud to yourself, "You know, I really am OK!"

Notice how your body and breathing feel. Do you take deeper, more relaxed breaths after OKing yourself? How does your voice sound? Is it deeper? Are your vocal cords more relaxed than usual?

Now do the opposite. Think of times when you've been criticized. Detail them, and after each say, "I know I'm not really OK." Check your physical signs now.

Remain alert to your body signs of OKness and not-OKness.

Transactional Analysis wants us to believe that we are really OK, that is, OK in an ultimate sense, that we have absolute value as persons. In offering complete OKness, TA is really offering us a form of salvation, a gospel to believe, and is therefore intensely religious. This religious aura that hangs over Transactional Analysis was revealed by Harris himself in an article in *Time* magazine:

> In fact, Harris is convinced that only those who believe the "truth" of Transactional Analysis can win the battle against neurosis. "You have to have absolute faith that TA is true; otherwise you'll lose, . . ." Speaking more than half seriously, he told one patient who had not read *I'm OK — You're OK* that "the only thing standing between you and a cure is my book." The book itself goes as far as to suggest that it may be able to save man and civilization from extinction.[9]

Transactional Analysis deals with religion and God as it deals with ultimate value, threat, and affirmation, but it finally cuts off this God-dimension because it does not push its understanding of man far enough. It does not question the source of the experience of ultimate not-OKness, nor does it question where its proclamation of absolute OKness is grounded. It also does not ask if and how these two sources are related to each other. It backs off from these questions and limits itself (as far as Christians, but probably not Harris, are concerned) to relative threat and limited self and interpersonal OKness.

It is perfectly possible, of course, for Transactional Analysis as a secular psychological technique to ignore where its understanding of man and its offer of OKness in the face of not-OKness ultimately lead. But Christians see Transactional Analysis in its proper limited role and consider questions that TA ignores.

Christianity is not in competition with Transactional Analysis at the point of an understanding of man which says man is not-OK, needs to be, and must become so if his life is to be whole and healthy. Christianity's concern is with

[9] "TA: Doing OK," *Time,* 20 August 1973, pp. 44 – 46.

how a man responds to this threat of not-OKness, and with what the source of a man's OKness is.

Picking ourselves up

The noted psychiatrist Paul Tournier sees self-justification as the universal problem, both social and religious, of mankind.[10] Here, however, Christianity takes issue with Transactional Analysis. Transactional Analysis says that healing comes when one realizes that the not-OK state is an illusion. It is only the result of one's outdated Parental "tapes." Salvation occurs when the Adult can update the tapes. It must be very clear what is meant here by illusion. Transactional Analysis views not-OKness as illusory (*feeling* not-OK is a genuine experience) in the sense that a man is really, ultimately OK. He only *feels* not-OK.

Christianity says that the not-OK state is real, but that our responses to it are illusions. The not-OK state has an all too frightening reality. Salvation comes not in denying its validity (making myself OK through an act of Adult will, really through self-absolution), but in accepting the not-OK state and my responsibility, giving up my illusory existence by which I live as if I were OK, and receiving the overwhelming, unconditional OK verdict offered in Jesus of Nazareth.

Grace is thus the reality of our being OKed by God's affirmation even when we do not feel or cannot make ourselves OK.

C. S. Lewis in *The Great Divorce* describes the illusions that men live by and by which they seek to defend themselves. Men build houses

[10] *Guilt and Grace: A Psychological Study* (London: Hodder and Stoughton, 1962), pp. 80 – 88.

that don't protect them from the elements, defenses that don't defend, securities that don't make secure, and in the midst of their illusions are in hell, out of touch with reality.

You probably haven't tried this lately. Make an old-fashioned house of cards — out of a deck of cards. Really. When you've finally gotten something together, imagine that you are small enough and light enough to live in it. You have to walk on the slippery floor. To get from one room to another you have to crawl over the cards. There is always a giant dog, cat, or child ready to knock your house down. There are no shades, no protection.

If nothing really comes along and knocks your house down while you're "in it," knock it down yourself.

Consider your own illusions and reality.

———

Another powerful statement of the human predicament is portrayed by Hannah Green in *I Never Promised You a Rosegarden*, in which a psychiatrist can only finally offer his patient reality with all its harshness and brutality, but which is still preferable to the illusory dream world of mental illness.

If you have not already read it, buy a copy or borrow one from your library. It is available in paperback.

In the area of the reality and unreality of the human situation Transactional Analysis shares the same flaw as most traditional psychiatry. Psychiatry says that a man should not feel guilty. He must recognize that he is not responsible. All of his behavior can be accounted for on the basis of childhood conditioning (Parent or superego) or sexual impulses (Child or id). (Although paradoxically psychiatry wants a man to take responsibility for himself in the healing process.) Perhaps the most radical statement of behavioristic determinism, of irresponsibility, is B. F. Skinner's *Beyond Freedom and Dignity.*

Despite his popularity, many psychologists feel Skinner has spent too much time with his rats, and one is reminded of the one rat who said to the other: "I've got my experimenter completely conditioned. Every time I ring the bell, he brings me food!"

Christianity, on the other hand, *deals* with guilt as a reality. Traditional psychiatry says, "You're not guilty, believe that! You only feel guilty." Christianity says, Accept your guilt as a reality; take responsibility for it, and receive God's acceptance in spite of judgment and guilt."

Transactional Analysis, in saying that a man is not really, ultimately *not*-OK, has a fundamentally different perception of reality from Christianity. A man in his totality is a responsible being. He cannot play off his Parent-self (conditioning) against his Child-self (instinct). Parent, Adult, and Child, the whole man stands before God either in illusion or truth, faith or unfaith, acknowledging the reality about himself or denying it.

Moralism — being good

This distinction between the view of Transactional Analysis and Christianity is not the error posed when Christianity is confused with morality.

Moralism is still an ever-present threat to the Gospel. For moralism short-circuits the Gospel by approaching Scripture not to find how it says the Gospel, but to derive applications from it for life. The Bible then becomes a compendium of moral teaching and Jesus the great moral teacher. Believing the Gospel becomes "following the teachings of Jesus," not entrusting ourselves to him in faith.

The Gospel, of course, is not without moral implications, but they come only out of believing the Gospel and then asking how one as a believer of the Gospel relates himself to the world and other men.

What is moralism?

Luke 18:18-30; Matt. 19:16-23 — A rich man comes to Jesus and asks, "Teacher, what must I do to have eternal life?" Jesus answers, "Sell what you possess and give to the poor, and you will have a treasure in heaven; and come, follow me."

1. Does Jesus mean that we ought not have too much money? **Yes No**
2. Does He mean that we shouldn't be so materialistic? **Yes No**
3. Is Jesus suggesting that the rich man's money is his idol? **Yes No**
4. Is Jesus suggesting that the rich man should get his security from Jesus and the Gospel? **Yes No**
5. Do we properly use the text when we, through it, expose and examine our own idols? **Yes No**
6. Does moralism here invite us to place our

48

trust in correct action rather than Jesus, the affirming Friend of sinners?   **Yes   No**

As you have probably guessed, the moralist would answer *yes* to the first two questions and *no* to the next four. The Christian would answer the opposite.

Misusing being good

For the man of unfaith Transactional Analysis can become just another way of establishing superiority, of OKing himself at the expense of others, of exploiting and manipulating. Harris speaks approvingly of a businessman who learned to close many deals by using his understanding of Transactional Analysis to appeal to the Parent or Child in the other man.[11]

While the Parent is an unabashed self-justifier who achieves his secure superiority by imposing rules and injunctions to establish an unassailable, impregnable position of OKness — and while the Child achieves security as the center of all, seeking to be served — the Adult, too, can be a self-justifier, albeit a more subtle one. To be sure, there is more hope for the Adult because this is where the "evaluative I" (the reasoning self-critic) and the Gospel operate.

Most often, however, we use this capacity for self-excuse, self-congratulation, or self-despair. The Adult is still confronted by the struggle between faith and unfaith. Moving from Parent or Child to Adult does not automatically guarantee complete and honest openness to one's fellows, nor removal of Parental (recognition of conditional not-OKness) or transcendent (recognition of unconditional not-OKness) guilt.

[11] Harris, pp. 93, 94.

You are a salesman (soap, deoderant, cars, jewelry, whatever) familiar with TA. Circle the behaviors that would best enable you to sell your product. Cross out those that wouldn't. Which attitudes would help salesman-you the most?

1. Be sensitive to the Child in others and "stroke" the Child — give it affirmation.
2. Address the Adult in your client.
3. Protect the Child in your client.
4. Let your client make a rational decision concerning your product.
5. Appreciate the need for the Child in others to express its creativity. Encourage that expression.
6. Encourage your client to reflect on his ultimate not-OKness, which no product can cover up.
7. Appreciate the need for the Child in others to unburden itself of its not-OKness.
8. Believe in the need to have an ethical framework that highlights your behavior and makes it look good.
9. Point out to your client that Christ, only, OKs him and that His OK is not an easy OK.
10. Know that TA is a good means of winning friends and influencing clients.

The salesman would circle one, three, five, seven, eight, and ten, and cross out the others. What do your choices on this little game say about TA's potential for manipulating others

56479

to your own ends and about the value of an "ethical system"?

The message of Jesus according to Harris is a "central historical example of I'm OK – You're OK [note that even Jesus is reduced to an example of Transactional Analysis] and the life-style of the apostles was based on I'm OK – You're OK.[12]

Harris seems to feel that Jesus went around telling people, "I'm OK – You're OK." Apparently he has never read Jesus' words to the pharisees or some of the sermons in Acts calling for repentance.

Of course Jesus, the Apostles, and Christians value people very highly and do their best to affirm and support others, but this never blunts the Christian belief that mankind is in need of salvation. Indulgently proclaiming "I'm OK – You're OK" without reference to an OKer or an event that makes OKness a possibility is merely perpetuating illusion, reinforcing the "as if" existence, and trivializing the words and actions of Jesus into what Bonhoeffer called "cheap grace," which is really no grace at all.

An episode in a TV comedy in which the star plays a psychologist portrayed the pathetically tenuous nature of illusory OK feelings. As long as his group-therapy group told each other they were OK, all was well. But when any one of the group expressed any kind of negative feelings, the whole group sank into instant despair and a turmoil of not-OK feelings.

[12] Ibid., p. 236.

51

Transactional Analysis cannot be extended beyond its own inherent validity as Harris does when he claims that TA is *the* solution to the problems of mankind, from the family to international relations. For the Adult state is just as capable of sin as the Parent or Child. Christians can stand with Luther at this point in feeling that reason can never substitute for OK affirmation as a gift of God.[13]

An answer

Remember the question we asked at the beginning of this chapter? What place is there for Transactional Analysis in pastoral counseling? And really in your life, Christian? Now, I think, we are prepared to give a serious and carefully considered answer.

Transactional Analysis offers an extremely useful and helpful tool for increasing one's self-understanding of the nature of personal dynamics and of interpersonal interaction. But for pastoral use it is necessary to incorporate P-A-C into a larger framework of counseling which includes sensitizing people to an awareness of the ways they defend and justify themselves at the expense of others. This is really to "do the Law," exposing sin, bad faith, misplaced trust, and false gospels, and to offer people Jesus of Nazareth as the Gospel to which to entrust themselves.

A doctor cannot treat an illness without first making a diagnosis. This is an important aspect of theology — to make a diagnosis of the human condition to which the Gospel is addressed.

This movement takes us from counseling to individual confession and absolution and into the heart of what makes Christian counseling and pastoral care unique. Here Chris-

[13] Brian Gerrish, *Grace and Reason: A Study in the Theology of Luther* (Oxford: Clarendon Press, 1962).

tianity and its Gospel stand above and beyond whatever counseling technique one may use. For personal use of Transactional Analysis by individual Christians, such honesty and openness is also essential in order that we may be "sinners in truth," confessing and redeemed sinners.

But since we are all so adept at self-deception, even and especially when we think we are most right and most honest, it is essential to place ourselves under pastoral care. Such pastoral care in the broadest sense is our ministry to one another, and it includes the admonition, criticism, encouragement, and concern of our husband, wife, family, friends, and associates, who are often in a position to know us much more intimately than pastors.

You may find the short book for laypeople *Forgiveness and Confession: the Keys to Renewal,* by Alvin Rogness (Augsburg, 1970), helpful in your self-examination.

5.

OF COURSE WE'RE GUILTY...

This chapter and the next concern themselves with the problem of guilt—your problem of guilt and mine—as it is understood by Freud, TA, and Christianity.

Freud and TA

The underlying goal of Transactional Analysis was to find a simplified vacabulary for traditional psychoanalytic terms, that could be readily understood and easily used by patients. This relationship can be seen in the following diagram.

The P-A-C model is based on the Freudian model. One difference is that the Freudian model is more concerned with what the ego states *are*, while TA is more concerned with what they *do*. For Transactional Analysis the ego states, the circles, are not just a theory; they can be demonstrated to exist. TA is a movement away from the theoretical level, toward the practical level.

Second and more important for the Christian, TA shifts its emphasis from the Freudian focus on sexuality and unconscious drives to man's values, his OKness and

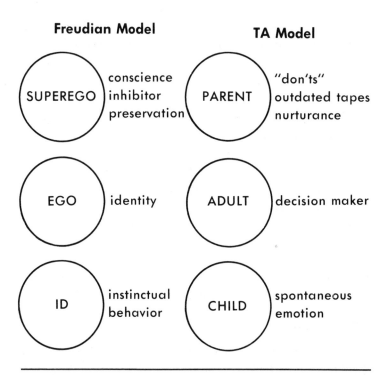

Freudian Model

TA Model

SUPEREGO — conscience, inhibitor, preservation

PARENT — "don'ts", outdated tapes, nurturance

EGO — identity

ADULT — decision maker

ID — instinctual behavior

CHILD — spontaneous emotion

not-OKness, and how he consciously verbalizes his feelings of worth.

There is also a similarity in method and goal between Freudian psychotherapy and TA. Each moves from gathering of awareness through growing awareness to full awareness. Each tries to produce a better, stronger leader in the Adult self or ego, one that recognizes and controls the games the other parts of the self play with it.

Freudian analysis takes years. It's a bit like an extensive archeological dig where you are the excavation site and the process is to uncover the runes of your younger years. Transactional Analysis is faster and uses your present expressions of Parent and Child (those evident in your current relationships) to quickly raise the level of your awareness and your ability to deal with your problems.

TA is less concerned with removing "hang-ups" than with learning how to live creatively with them.

In addition, TA is concerned that we take responsibility for our situations. Christians might well rejoice to hear that.

But if we have unlimited freedom for change, we need not feel guilt: we can improve our former unhappy lots and can on our own achieve the OKness and the forgiveness we seek. Our "backs are not against the wall," and we are not in need of the kind of radical alternative offered by the Christian faith. We are not guilty! (It should be noted, however, that recently TA has become less optimistic about the possibilities of boundless change.)

What is guilt?

Guilt is a fact and it is a feeling. It is the fact of having committed a breach of conduct involving a penalty. It is being culpable. It is also the feeling of culpability—the sensation of shattered responsibility. It is a consequence of sin. A person does something wrong and feels bad about it. Sin is being guilty and sin causes feelings of guilt.

But sin is not really a social term. It is a theological one describing man's relation to God.

In John Milton's great epic of sin and grace, *Paradise Lost*, Satan, the most magnificent of the angels, falls when he sees his position threatened by God. He knows he is not the brightest star in the heavens and feels threatened by that knowledge. That is sin. In other words, he eats of the tree of knowledge and knows God as threat. He then tempts man as he tempted himself. And man hides from an all-threatening God.

Sin is the opposite of trusting in Christ's affirmation. Sin is the activity of self-justification rather than trusting in God to be our justifier, our affirmer.

Sin, violating our relationship of trust with God, has antisocial, illegal, and immoral consequences.

For example if a man places his trust in wealth to provide his affirmation as well as his meaning for existing, then this is his sin in the theological sense. It is getting the good news, the OK for his life, from a false, creaturely value which has been elevated to the position of highest concern, rather than from God's Good Word about Him in Jesus.

This sin has its immediate behavioral consequences: Such a person may see material things as more important than people and as a result will use and exploit others to "make it to the top of the ladder." Perhaps he will even be driven to engage in illegal and immoral activities to get that wealth, to serve his "god."

A British journalist described the president of a gigantic international conglomerate as a manic, driven man with the glint in his eyes of a pirate, running roughshod over social, human, and political values with the attitude that what's good for the company is good for the world.

Guilt also has a theological and a behavioral component. A person may feel guilt over his antisocial, illegal, or immoral actions and never feel or even recognize that he has sinned. He may not know that he has been engaged in bad faith, misplaced trust, and self-justification, nor recognize that he is responsible before the Author of his existence. Guilt caused by behavior (a psychological problem) is closely related to culpability, the theological problem of being responsible for not trusting in God.

We all feel accountable for our lives. We all feel that we are held responsible by a lord. Isn't that feeling apparent every day in our desperate need to be always right, to prove ourselves, our actions, and ultimately our total existence? Government officials, too, justify whatever actions, legal or illegal, on the grounds of national security. Rebels kill and burn in the name of peace and justice. This behavior is a universally distinguishable phenomenon of human existence.

Consider Mr. Always-Right. He rarely, if ever, loses an argument. Even when the evidence begins to stack up against him, he can salvage respect for his position. He acts doubly certain in order to guard against demoralizing doubt. Basically, his self-esteem is threatened. He has deep doubts about himself.

Now study each of the following statements. After meditation, circle T or F for each. This is a form of confession.

1. I am accountable and responsible for my life.   T F
2. I am threatened by that experience.   T F
3. If I were innocent, I should be happy to give an account of myself.   T F
4. Because I am not happy to account for my life, I see my culpability.   T F
5. Because I feel responsible and not right, like a child I try to excuse myself and make

myself right to my world and to my God
T F
6. This attempt at "righting" is my sin of unbelief. **T F**
7. Because of my unbelief I raise up relative values and worship false gods. **T F**
8. And so I feel guilty, for to elevate some human values, I always cancel others.
T F

These are the dynamics of religious and social guilt. This need for justification is the source of our self-made religion. For we are not satisfied with partial affirmation; we want ultimate affirmation of the totality of our existence. Therefore we make godlike demands on that which affirms us. We want an ultimate "yes," and this enslaves us to our gods. We act as though whatever confers godlike affirmation on us is all that really counts, and we will sacrifice anything else for it. Man needs affirmation, looks for it, and gives ultimacy to that which affirms him.

The roots of guilt

For further analysis of guilt we need to look at two more aspects: how it is rooted in our values, and how it is rooted in time. (Compare the following to T. Oden, *The Structure of Awareness,* Abingdon, 1969.)

All of us have a system of values, such as friendship, loyalty, health, honesty, family, home, property, education, recreation, peace, government, and country. These values are formed and influenced by our culture, education, parents, socio-economic status, religion, and other factors. They also align themselves in a pyramid effect, where some are of greater and others of lesser importance. It is a basic psychological principle that we act primarily on the basis of our values. Values determine and shape behavior.

Guilt results from those situations in which we are forced to choose among our values. Because these values are important and give meaning to us, we cannot deny them without incurring guilt.

If a man who values peace and puts a high value on the life and worth of each human being is forced to kill another in a war, he must incur guilt, no matter how valid that particular war may be. He is forced to sacrifice one value for another. Thus guilt is an inevitable partner in the human situation, lurking as a shadow as we move among our value choices. For every value affirmation involves a concommitant value negation. This is what question eight in the last box refers to.

If, as with Dr. Skinner, you save your book instead of your children and you value both, then you have affirmed the value of the one and negated the other, with the inevitable result of conscious or unconscious guilt.

While the choice made in this example is highly irresponsible, it is nevertheless not as farfetched as it seems. We all know the guilt of parents whose children have gotten into trouble because the parents were too busy with business or social affairs to give them the kind of guidance necessary. Here a value choice was made with the resulting consequences. Guilt, then, is tied to values.

Draw your own value pyramid. Place your highest value (that which you consider the most important in your life, that which you would be least willing to give up) on the top line. For example, your highest value could be realizing your own potential. Then work your way down. On the same line place those values that you could not easily choose between.

We will refer to your value pyramid again.

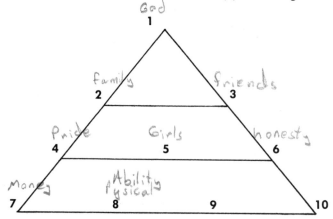

Second, guilt is tied to time. We can only feel guilty about those values we have already negated, that is, those in the past. Our access to the past is memory. But memory is not an absolutely reliable record, such as a film or tape. It is constantly being modified and influenced by present thinking, activity, and experience. Thus a painful, guilt-incurring activity can become in the protective, illusion-creating function of memory more positive and possibly even attractive with the passage of time. A married man's affair, which was painful and guilt producing at the time and which hurt his marriage, can appear through the filter of time to have been an exciting, even desirable, romantic liaison.

Guilt is the awareness of value negation in the past which is accessible through memory. Guilt can result from responsible negation in a forced-choice situation among values of equal validity. So guilt does not come only from irresponsible choices.

Since values are very personal and uniquely conditioned by our individual experience, it is clear that one man's values are not necessarily anothers. The unity and cohesiveness of a group or society depends a great deal on the extent of mutually shared values. Society provides overarching values that can be accepted and shared by its members.

It is just such authority (commonly shared allegiance to a system of overarching values) that seems to be breaking down in contemporary society. The result is fragmentation into polarized groups which each have their own values and meanings. One man may feel guilt over actions that another would not. A ghetto gang member may feel guilt in turning in others for wrong doing since the value his group places on "not squealing" is very high. Another, conditioned by an atmosphere that prizes individualism, may feel this is a perfectly appropriate and responsible action.

Anxiety

Anxiety is on the other side of the coin from guilt. It is oriented toward the future, in which through imagination we become aware of possible threats to values considered necessary for our existence. We become aware of the possibility of value negation in the future.

Our house may burn down, our stocks may fall, our job may be lost. But what separates legitimate concern for the future from neurotic anxiety is once again the religious dimension revealed in values and value choices.

If, for example, we invest godlike value in our children, if they are our highest worth, then we fear the loss or failure of that god and cannot allow our children to do anything that might be dangerous. We become overprotective, or we may be unable to admit that they could do anything wrong or bad.

We all know the terrible anxiety that some mothers feel when their last child is about to marry and leave home if they made the care and nurturance of that child their sole reason for existing.

Or a man may face retirement with great fear and anxiety and possibly die of a heart attack shortly after leaving work because his job was the only thing that meant anything to him.

If we invest youth with highest value (as our culture seems to), then we become fanatical (and ridiculous) in our pursuit of youth and longevity while denying the value of age, maturity, wisdom, and experience.

Think of some of the women you have seen in bikinis at the beach, and try to imagine the kind of illusions they must have about themselves!

Bodies sag; health is good, but sickness comes; children are a pleasure, but they grow up and leave; marriage can be beautiful, but it is at best bittersweet, for the dearer my spouse is to me the more agonizing will be the final separation. Life is dear, but it too passes with time. And in the end our self-made gods come crashing down around us.

They will fail us, for they are not what we have made them out to be. They have failed to give us the ultimate affirmation we invested them with. This is why neither time nor history is redemptive. Things do not get better and better all the time.

Read the dialog in the Appendix, p. 118. It describes a conversation between a taxi driver and a pastor. In a way the driver is all of us. How many of his views do you share? How would you respond to the pastor?

As you read, cover the remainder of the page with a piece of paper, moving it gradually down the page. When you come to a line in the margin, stop. Cover up what follows, and write down on a separate piece of paper what you expect to be the next response and how you would respond. Check yourself, and read until you come to another line. Then guess again.

This exercise is designed to sharpen your ability to empathize and is a check on how you're doing with this chapter.

The results of guilt

That we are at the same time both victims and responsible is the tragedy of the human situation. If we were innocent, we would only be pathetic victims of persecution. If we were not accountable, we would be only pathetic victims of fate. But the truly tragic character of human existence is that we are bound to need to be OK; we are bound to seek OKness, and we make what OKs us our God. At the same time we know we are held responsible for those very actions of idolatry by which we attempt to OK ourselves and are forced to admit that responsibility.

No wonder men are driven to despair and the frantic pursuit of something to comfort and affirm them in the face of this threatening responsibility. It seems outrageous that we should both be victims of fate and destiny and be held responsible.

This tragic character of human existence, the paradox of the guilty victim, is depicted in tragic works of literature such as *Oedipus Rex, Macbeth,* and Kafka's *The Trial.* In these literary works the tragic protagonist is portrayed as a fated man, destined to doom (victim), but also as one who makes his fate his own by the choices he makes which are guilt incurring (responsible). Throughout these works the characters' self-justifications and self-deceptions are revealed, but in the end their innate sense of accountability and guilt comes increasingly to the fore, recognized in the tragic moment when their last defenses break down and they are faced with the full realization of their mistakes, responsibility, and guilt.

Sometimes that realization leads to an affirmation of nothingness or, as we have earlier described it, to a realization of God as threat only.

At the end of *Macbeth* (V, v, 17 — 28), his wife just having killed herself, Macbeth asserts most eloquently this affirmation of nothingness, in one of Shakespeare's most famous speeches:

She should have died hereafter:
There would have been a time for such a word.
Tomorrow, and tomorrow, and tomorrow,
Creeps in this petty pace from day to day
To the last syllable of recorded time;
And all our yesterdays have lighted fools
The way to dusty death. Out, out, brief candle!
Life's but a walking shadow, a poor player
That struts and frets his hour upon the stage
And then is heard no more. It is a tale
Told by an idiot, full of sound and fury,
Signifying nothing.

The judgmental consequences of sin (broken relationships) are already built into the structures of existence. They are part of the order of things. Sin brings its own punishment. God does not need to add anything. If in the attempt to justify myself, to prove my rightness and superiority (sin), I beat my wife, then the consequence is that I have a wife who remembers being beaten, and a primary relationship is broken. If a fine of 60 days in jail could remove the memory which stands forever between the two, it would be well worth it.

Retribution and punishment are built into the structure of existence; they are part of the experience of threat. Punishment doesn't require God's additional intervention into things, but forgiveness does. In Jesus we have God the Forgiver becoming part of our history, breaking the cycle of retribution by absorbing the hurt rather than passing it on.

The Fall account in Genesis 3 can summarize much of what has been said about sin, self-justification, threat, and the consequences. Temptation comes through the serpant and the woman, but Adam accedes to it. Sin comes both from outside us (we are victims), and at the same time from within (we are responsible).

This deliberate pictorial paradox describes the tragic nature of the human situation, the guilty victim. The fall occurs because man is jealous of God. He wants to be his own God, his own vindicator, defender, and affirmer. Sin is this assertion of independence and self-sovereignty. It is a denial of our creatureliness and of the sovereignty of God.

The story of Adam is the story of mankind. It is our story. In this intensely psychological description the concern is not only to describe Adam's experience, but to show our own reliving of Adam's experience. In this fall we relive our own feelings of estrangement and how all of our relationships are messed up.

Finally weeds grow in the garden, and in guilt Adam blames Eve. She blames the serpent, and they both blame God. This is a reliving of the rebellion and its consequences in which we all participate. We transgress because we want to. And we do it with the knowledge that it will destroy us. But we do it anyway and try to get out of the consequences by excusing ourselves and blaming others.

The message of the Fall account is that we are a fallen people. Sin is the universal habit of mankind. Our moral goodness is relative and socially determined, but our sinfulness before God is absolute.

Redemption is found only in trusting the experience of being vindicated, being OKed, by God as the last word about us, the final, decisive verdict on our lives, rather than trusting threat as the last word. This affirmation is grounded in the event of Jesus of Nazareth as the vindicator who was experienced in history and who, in our trusting of the proclamation about Him, the Good News, is experienced in our history. We want and need an ultimate YES in our lives in the face of the inescapable threatening NO that hangs over us. This YES is found in Jesus. Our OKness is grounded there!

For the Son of God, Jesus Christ, whom we preached among you, Silvanus and Timothy and I, was not YES and NO; but in him it is always YES. For all the promises of God find their YES in Him, to the glory of God. (2 Cor. 1:19-20)

This is the only YES that sustains us as we live out our lives within structures of existence that proclaim a constant NO to us. This YES of God is believed against the NO evidence of our experience of the threatening void.

Sin and moral transgression are closely bound up with each other as are responsibility and guilt. Thus in reality the religious and the psychological are inexorably bound together. The gap between religion and experienced reality, between faith and life-experience in the secular polarization is really a false one.

6.

BUT MUST WE REMAIN GUILTY?

The treatment of guilt

Three points concerning the nature and dynamics of guilt lay the groundwork for a Gospel proclamation that accounts for our real guilt and offers a therapy that effects genuine healing — an alternative to the temporal healing of Transactional Analysis.

I. It is possible to *be* guilty (culpable) without *feeling* guilty.

II. Psychologically it is possible to feel guilty unconsciously without consciously recognizing it. This dynamic is intensely religious in nature.

Many patients are astonished when their psychologist or psychiatrist tells them that they have guilt feelings (which the psychologist has seen coming out in such behavior as alchoholism or drug addiction by which they are unconsciously punishing themselves for their guilt). Often such patients will deny any guilt. Their behavior must be caused by something else. This is an attempt to preserve the illusion of innocence and blamelessness about themselves which is a self-justifying attempt to deny responsibility and accountability. This repressed guilt is denied and can surface in other damaging psychological problems.

A man feeling guilty over an affair may become impotent with his wife and deny all the while to his counselor that he feels guilty about anything, while his inner guilt has surfaced as a psychosomatic malady. We strive by our denials to preserve the illusion of blamelessness, while deep down inside the seeds of repressed guilt are growing, waiting to burst to the surface at any time, often in ways and forms we least expect. This is why guilt is so destructive.

III. The recognition of guilt is not redemptive. Admitting a crime does not exonerate that criminal act. In fact, it is often little more than the substitution of one problem for another as one moves from self-deception (denial of responsibility) to despair (recognition of the responsibility).

In therapy this recognition is often called catharsis, the emotional release accompanying the confrontation of truth and recognition of responsibility. This is a goal of psychotherapy.

Psychology then seeks to move to a third phase, resolution, in which the patient moves from despair over admitted responsibility and guilt, to bearing and overcoming that guilt by feeling that in the acceptance of guilt and in spite of it one is really OK after all. This psychological procedure can be diagrammed as follows:

| 3. *self-acceptance* (resolution) |
| 2. *self-discovery* (catharsis, resulting in initial despair) |
| 1. *self-deception* (recognized in dysfunctional neuroses) |

Psychologically this process is seen as a linear movement from one state to another new one. Theologically, however, this process is circular.

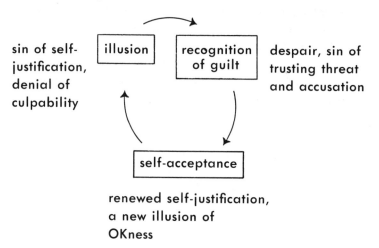

sin of self-justification, denial of culpability — illusion → recognition of guilt — despair, sin of trusting threat and accusation → self-acceptance →

renewed self-justification, a new illusion of OKness

Theologically the third stage is a new form of self-vindication whereby one has moved from the position of victimized innocence and denial of responsibility (stage one) to the position of OKness by accepting responsibility, which is in reality another illusory self-affirmation. For as we said, the recognition of guilt is not redemptive. We are not OKed by the act of admitting our guilt. This is confession with self-absolution, which is no absolution at all.

Poor Me

Like other favorite games, this is really an an attempt to "con" and manipulate others. It is an endless admission of guilt with no absolution. Indeed, real absolution would end the game!

Its real purpose is to prove I'm not-OK. Then to enjoy the misery of it all. It does, however, give evidence of our negative feelings about ourselves.

Psychology tells us how important self-acceptance is. Theology does not deny this but asks on what basis does a man accept himself. Where does he get the feeling that he is OK? What is the source of his affirmation? Theology here offers a different alternative from psychology's. The pastoral counselor and the Christian need to be aware of it. The Christian faith offers that self-acceptance which comes from trusting that God accepts me.

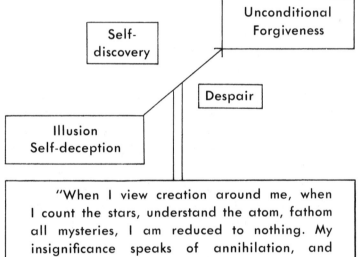

Self-discovery	Unconditional Forgiveness
Despair	
Illusion Self-deception	

"When I view creation around me, when I count the stars, understand the atom, fathom all mysteries, I am reduced to nothing. My insignificance speaks of annihilation, and I fear. It is revealed to me that I am a nobody. But in this fear I find strength. My entire confidence hinges on the author of life and through faith in him I know I am a somebody! [14]

[14] Paul Johnson, *Personality and Religion* (Nashville: Abingdon Press, 1957), p. 20.

This form of self-acceptance is offered as an alternative to the self-acceptance that comes from saying I'm OK *because* I admit my guilt (a form of self-justification seen even in confession, where a man may say, "At least I admit my sins," meaning "I'm OK because I'm better than others").

We call those who think they are better than others and who put on airs, phonies. The Christian is OK and can accept himself without despair and affirm his worth not *because* he admits his guilt, but *in spite of* guilt and sin.

When we

EXPERIENCE

being "worthed" by God — accepted, affirmed, and OKed — we can live without despair in the face of acknowledged guilt and responsibility. This is the meaning of the forgiveness of sins: to live with a guilty past without despair or self-justifications which result in fanaticism.

The TA myth

Fanaticism occurs in counseling when the patient becomes absolutely dependent on the counselor because the counselor affirms, accepts, and tells the patient he is OK. Paul Tillich has said that this total accepting affirmation by a counselor is a contemporary secular expression of grace. But what counselor can accept us unconditionally?

Consider the danger. Often the patient comes to hang on every word, expression, gesture, and action of the counselor and grants him godlike authority. Then when the humanness of the counselor is seen or a hint of criticism, judgment, or nonacceptance drops, the relation is shattered. Such occasions throw the overdependent patient into a tizzy of self-doubt and despair.

The affirmation of the counselor can be an efficacious expression of grace if it is affirmation in the name of Jesus, that is, if it points beyond the human mediator with his relative, though valuable, acceptance to the ultimate, unconditional affirmation of God in Jesus, which is utterly reliable and trustworthy and will not let us down or fail us.

The Christian counselor is in a unique position to offer the alternative of faith in God's activity in Jesus rather than faith and trust in self-affirmation, the counselor's affirmation, or the despair that results from trusting in threat. The Christian is in the unique position to be aware that neither he, himself, nor his counselor is God and that the OKness offered by the counselor or by Transactional Analysis is only a relative, limited interpersonal "type" or representation of the transpersonal, ultimate OK offered us when we trust in Jesus as God the affirmer.

For these reasons Christians must be conscious and critical of the understanding of man and the type and limitations of the OKness offered by Transactional Analysis. The diagram on page 75 shows the respective operative fields of both Transactional Analysis and Christianity.

Christians need such an awareness as this because TA does not seem to recognize its own limitations. In its enthusiastic missionary zeal it does not acknowledge its relativity. Christians must recognize, if Transactional Analysis will not, that what it sees of the experience of man is only a partial abstraction of the whole of the human situation. The OKness Transactional Analysis offers is only a part of what a man needs; it is only a part of what is

	TA			Christianity
	I recognize that I stand under relative threat.	**NOT OK**		I recognize my absolute not-OKness as I experience my day-by-day not-OKness. I recognize God as my just accuser.
	I recognize my possibilities for improving my interpersonal relationships (my relative OKness).	**OK**		I experience my ultimate OKness in my relation to God when I trust Jesus' affirmation. He is the friend of sinners. My values shift and my interpersonal relations change. I experience God as forgiver.

necessary for us to be truly OK.

In *this* form, Transactional Analysis is a denial of the Christian faith and needs to be recognized, confronted, and rejected by Christians as a heretical false Gospel (without at the same time rejecting its more limited legitimate use). For as we have seen, Transactional Analysis sees healing not as redemption, the radical shifting of trust, but largely as self-enlightenment, as an education enterprise in which Childhood ignorance is replaced by Adult wisdom.

In this process Jesus takes his place among history's other great teachers of wisdom, offering a set of ethical principles by which to live. Harris even goes as far as to equate his prized position of I'm OK—You're OK with grace. Harris says, "You are accepted unconditionally." [15] Again our questions arise: But by whom? And how? For Christian use it seems that a massive "demythologization" of the salvation pretensions of Transactional Analysis must take place so that it does not compromise the Christian faith.

> One way of demythologizing a myth is to make it more clearly mythical.

> Try writing the myth of how TA saved the world. "Once upon a time . . ." might be a good beginning. Then create an evil foe (a dragon, vicious being, etc.), a destroying bondage, prisoners, a TA hero, and a saving action. Try to include in your myth as much of TA as you know. Make it vivid and dramatic.

> Read your myth to friends and discuss it.

At the point of guilt, theology and TA psychology have two different perceptions of its nature, extent, and healing. Harris puts Transactional Analysis above religion and perhaps correctly criticizes churches for being "Parental" (authoritarian). He also seeks to understand religion in terms of the dynamics of Transactional Analysis, thus in effect reducing religious (for example, Christian) perceptions of reality to a dynamic of his own. Harris makes ethics the point of contact with religion. This is inadequate, for as we have seen, it mislocates the real concerns of Christianity.

Idols

All of this has been a discussion of some of the dynamics of guilt. We have also seen how values and value choices reveal the religious dimension of human existence.

[15] Harris, p. 227.

Indeed, our god is that value we give highest worth in our life at any one moment. We normally have a pantheon of highest values (gods) and shift our trust among them as one or another fails us. Highest values are revealed in crisis situations where we are forced to choose.

If we make a god out of our country, we then justify all that our country does whether or not it is wrong according to our other values. If we make a god out of health, we become health faddists or hypochondriacs, who live in perpetual fear of germs. If we make a god out of pleasure, we become self-centered hedonists and gluttonous consumers.

We need to recognize and expose the contemporary idolatries in which so many of us trust and live. Is it really "in God we trust," or in the gross national product? Reading about idols of wood and stone in the Bible should not cause us to smugly chuckle at the naiveté and stupidity of "primitive" man, but it should cause us to explore and expose our own idolatries.

The story of temptation, pursuit of power, self-justification, and mutual accusation in Genesis 3 is not merely a cute myth about what happened way back then, once upon a time. Rather it is our story, yours and mine. It is the story of a fallen mankind and the sins we all share and suffer from. It is the pain we inflict on one another in our attempts to get out from under threat and make ourselves OK, even at the expense of others. We feel trapped and bound by our fate and destiny; we are caught up in the web of a guilty past, an empty present, and a threatening future. We need something in which to trust that will not desert us, grow old, decay, die, or fade away with the vicissitudes of time and history.

Our country can err, and its leaders can betray us. Our health can fail. Our money, goods, and pleasures can be lost. And despair results when our gods come crashing down around us. We have seen that none of the values we select as highest value are capable of being the highest value in our life. They cannot be extended beyond their own good and legitimate use. As gods, therefore, they are illusions. They cannot deliver the ultimate kind of affirmation we ask of them.

Here is a poem by a 12-year-old. It is a poignant example of man's need for affirmation. Its transparency makes us want to laugh and then weep—for in this child we are apt to see ourselves.

Me

They say I'm a chicken
But I'm really tough.
They say my punches are weak
But they're really rough.
They say I'm going to be a midget
But I'm really going to be big.
They say I cannot carry six pounds
But they don't know I could carry 100.
They say it takes a year for me to run a block
But it really takes me about five seconds.
They say I'm going to die at eighteen
But I think I'm going to die at forty-seven.
They say I never find money
But one day I found $25.15.

—Miquel Lopez [16]

[16] Kenneth Koch and the Students of P. S. 61 in New York City, *Wishes, Lies, and Dreams.* Copyright © 1970 by Kenneth Koch. Reprinted by permission of Random House, Inc.

Freedom in spite of guilt

Christianity, in contrast, offers another alternative, the good news that we have been affirmed not by illusion but by reality itself—the God beyond the gods. This affirmation took place not in some ethereal, supernatural, spirit world, but in the history of Jesus of Nazareth, the embodiment of forgiving love.

When we shift our trust to faith in Jesus as the alternative to the gods, we have a qualitatively different affirmation that leads not to self-justifying fanaticism or despair, but to freedom. This is freedom for repentance, freedom for responsibility, freedom from illusion and self-deception, and freedom for servanthood. It is the qualitatively different kind of freedom that comes when God supports us and not we our gods. This is forgiveness in spite of responsibility and guilt. It is the experience and awareness of the God beyond the gods.

It is here and only here that the so-called "attributes" of God make any sense. They are not the absurd, abstract philosophical speculations on the nature and being of God that they become when they are divorced from a Gospel context. Rather they are proclamations of how the Gospel is a qualitatively different kind of affirmation in time and history from the false gospels we trust in.

God is eternal. His affirmation does not leave, desert, or fail us. It outlasts time and history and our gods, which end and are as forgotten as yesterday's hero or deflated cause.

God is unchangeable. We can depend on His affirmation and promises. They won't let us down or turn against us.

God is omnipotent. He has the power to bring to pass what He has promised. His word is self-authenticating; it does what it says. It brings down the proud and arrogant and raises up the weak, despairing sinner in truth.

These are statements of grace, affirmation, love, and trustworthiness. They are statements of the Gospel in time and history. They are descriptions of the value, meaning, and affirmation that will last beyond time and history and that can free us from a threatening future. In this sense Jesus can say, "Take no thought for the morrow." He is not saying that we shouldn't have legitimate concern for the future, but rather that the love and affirmation of God which He bears can free us from neurotic anxiety and the failure of our gods. The future, as are we, is in God's hands.

What guilt really calls for is a "functional confessional." This has already been mentioned as an important direction for the church, its pastors, and members as they seek a uniquely Christian quality in pastoral counseling and in their personal use of psychology. David Belgum's comment deserves to be widely heard:

> Jesus said that if someone asks you for bread, it would be unthinkable to give him a stone. When persons suffering from the many painful and debilitating consequences of guilt come to the church for healing, they must be taken seriously and treated effectively. If the church cannot minister effectively at this point, there is little point in a big "turnout" Sunday morning for casual worship.[17]

For self-examination look at your pyramid of values. What does your pyramid look like? What values are on top? Have any recent crises or forced choices revealed them? Are these the ones that should be on top, that you want on top? Is your job, for example, more

[17] P. 118; see also pp. 119–41.

important than your family? Does your pyramid need rebuilding? Think about this list. Remember, values determine behavior. We act on what we believe and value.

You can reorder your values and alter the way you act. Discuss your values with your wife, husband, and children. Do you place the same importance on the same values? Differing values between husbands and wives, parents and children, can cause great difficulties in marriage and family. Should that bonus go for new shoes for the kids or for those golf clubs? What is the importance of hair length or the value of extreme cleanliness? Try to work out compromises if your pyramids don't match.

Look at your past. Have you engaged in value negations that have resulted in guilt? These are especially painful if they were irresponsible. This process of self-examination requires a great deal of honesty, self-awareness, and openness to the truth about yourself.

Remember that none of the values you have negated are God. If you trust His love and His affirmation, you can be free to face and examine these negations and to live with the hurt and painful consequences of past actions without despair.

What anxieties do you feel? What do you think threatens your future? Is the anxiety you feel normal concern or is it all out of proportion? This may reveal values you are overprotecting and investing with too ultimate a worth.

Take these troubling guilts, value negations, and severe anxieties to your pastor. Remember that he is not there to judge you but to aid your search for self-truth and to offer you the Gospel in which to place your trust. Discuss your concerns with him. This is called confession, but don't let that word scare you off.

It is necessary to be relieved of these burdens and to be offered the assurance and affirmation of the Gospel that will allow you to be free. Don't think that you don't need it or that you are too proud to admit that you are wrong. This is the self-justifying pride of the pharisaic sinners that Jesus condemned. Admit being a sinner. The friend of sinners loves you. Be affirmed!

Perhaps you may want to use the following form in your confession:

Conf.: Please hear my confession and declare that my sins are forgiven.
Pastor: Proceed.
Conf.: I confess my sins of unfaith before God. I confess all the false gospels I have trusted in, my pride, in which I have trusted in myself and self-contrived comforts, my rebellion and turning away, and my despair in the face of the affirmation and promises of the Gospel. (Specific elaboration may be made here.)
"Create in me a clean heart, O God, and renew a right spirit in me. Cast

me not away from Your presence and take not Your Holy Spirit from me. Restore unto me the joy of Your salvation, and uphold me with Your free spirit!"

Pastor: Do you confess that it is your nature to have bad faith, false gospels, and illusory hopes?

Conf.: Yes, I do!

Pastor: Do you acknowledge that these self-contrived gospels have resulted in brokenness within yourself, in your despair, fears, and anxieties? And in the violations of your neighbor, in defensiveness, anger, and mistrust?

Conf.: Yes, I do!

Pastor: Are you participating in the baptismal life-style and the continuing struggle to give up this bad faith and misplaced trust, instead trusting entirely in the love and mercy of God in Jesus.

Conf.: Yes, I am.

Pastor: Do you believe that the forgiveness I declare to you is the forgiveness of God.

Conf.: Yes, I do.

Pastor: Be it done for you as you have believed. According to the command of our Lord Jesus Christ, I forgive you your sins in the name of the Father, and of the Son, and of the Holy Spirit. Amen. Go and live out His peace!

7.
THE WAY WE ARE

TA can be constructively used by Christians. But as we have noted, it has limitations and pretensions. When it offers itself as a "salvation," as a gospel, it compromises the Christian faith.

A Christian can use TA by combining the dynamics of the Parent, Adult, and Child ego-states with an understanding of the truth-destroying and other-destroying nature of self-justification and defensiveness. We live under threat and need affirmation.

A Christian can use TA when he realizes that the Christian faith is a part of "lived" reality. The Gospel liberates and affirms each of us. We no longer need destructive self-justifications. We interact through the Gospel by repenting, admitting guilt without despairing, giving up illusions and self-deceptions, and creating more responsible value choices.

Chapters 2 through 6 have been an attempt to see TA and its understanding of man in the light of Christian theology and its Gospel. Much of this has, of necessity, been critical. This chapter is concerned with how TA can be of value to you, Christian, in helping you understand how God's judgment and affirmation can be seen to operate in your three ego states, Adult, Child, and Parent.

Society, civilization, and nature

Modern man is caught in a web of four patterns: anger, disesteem and self-hatred, guilt, and death.[18] Using the Transactional Analysis model of Parent, Adult, and Child, this predicament is the result of the Adult being caught in tension between competing demands of Parent and Child.

Consider carefully the following dilemma that drives man to disesteem:

"Civilization must not only restrain, it must give ideals, aims, goals, and models by which we are to be measured, stretched, and judged. And the higher the ideals, the greater the judgment. . . . Under such arduous demands, I look in the mirror and do not like what I see — a walking lie, a hypocrite. If I try to escape this bind by lowering my standards and ideals . . . then I look in the mirror and see a person with low standards, low ideals, and of course, low esteem."[19]

The triple dynamic of the individual self also exists on the larger scale of the group or society:

[18] Much of this material summarizes Christopher Allison, *Guilt, Anger, and God: The Pattern of Our Discontents* (New York: Seabury Press, 1972).

[19] Ibid., p. 9.

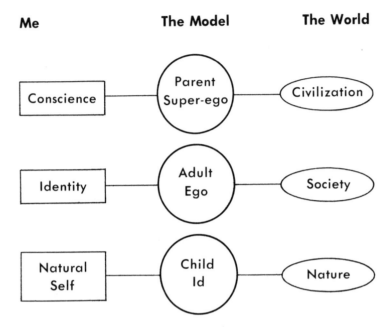

Me	The Model	The World
Conscience	Parent Super-ego	Civilization
Identity	Adult Ego	Society
Natural Self	Child Id	Nature

How is this conflict to be resolved? Most solutions offer a choice: Either opt for civilization (the Parent) or nature (the Child):

> "The contemporary hopes for solution to the human problem continue to follow, in general direction, the pattern of [Sigmund] Freud or [D. H.] Lawrence — toward greater or lesser structures of civilization. . . . Thus disesteem and guilt are resolved by sacrificing man's humanity. Anger and death are overcome by succumbing to them. Man still finds himself caught in the web of his discontents." [20]

How does Christianity face this option? It does not choose either civilization or nature; it offers a third choice — redemption or rebirth:

[20] Ibid., p. 32.

"This rebirth must be in the ego, [the Adult] the self's center. . . . Civilization is to Christianity as the Law is to the Gospel. . . . The Law is holy, just, and good, but it is the strength of sin. Similarly civilization is just such a good thing, but it also gives power to neuroses, self-damage, ill-health, and tends to repress the human spirit." [21]

Using this framework, sin becomes disesteem or self-hatred. The Gospel restores self-esteem, allowing us to respond to demands and yet retain wholeness. Self-righteousness will not heal disesteem. We cannot trust in civilization. Neither can we flee to nature. Christianity offers cosmic approval beyond this forced choice.

The Gospel offers us a third option beyond either law or license, in theological categories, and beyond civilization (Parent) or nature (Child), in psychological categories.

Threatened man

But sin isn't really disesteem. Sin is a relational term; it is responding to the threat of not-OKness by OKing ourselves, by self-justifying behavior that breaks relationships in all of life. Disesteem or self-hatred is the consequence of sin, not the definition of sin.

Similarly, restoration of self-esteem is not the Gospel, it is a result of the Gospel. The Gospel offers a new form of justification—God's—in place of self-justification. The transcendent affirmation of God lies in Jesus of Nazareth.

This is a little story about looking at the world through different kinds of holes:
"Once there was a school where they went out a lot to look at things. They could not afford cameras, so they cut

[21] Ibid., p. 42.

holes in paper to look through. The large holes were for long shots. The little holes were for close-ups.

They are surprised at how much they can see through the holes. The holes for close-ups wore out first. They say they could see more through the tiny hole."

— Herbert Brokering
"I" Opener: 80 Parables (CPH)

Pretend you have a sheet of paper with three different kinds of holes — one called Civilization, one called Nature, and one called Gospel. How big is each? How is each shaped? Is one filled with colored glass? If so, what color?

Look at the following scenes through each imaginary hole. Describe how the scene looks and changes.

1. A polluted Chicago skyline
2. Fishermen on Crane Lake in northern Minnesota
3. A large city library's reference room
4. A New York City jail
5. A group of teen-age lovers at a party
6. A young woman cooking supper for her family
7. Children playing in a park

Now try your magic sheet on some of your own scenes.

We do not OK ourselves; the "you're OK" verdict is conferred on us as a gift of God in Jesus.

If our devaluation of ourselves is a consequence of being caught between the demands of civilization and nature, between Parent and Child, then our role is passive;

we are acted on by forces outside our control, and we can "cop out." We aren't really responsible.

But if our root experience is threat, then we are thrust into an active role; we respond to threat through our Parent, Adult, and Child.

First, threat to our Adult results in despair and the experience of fate. We feel that not-OKness is both inevitable and unavoidable.

Second, threat to our Parent results in pride. We feel we can make ourselves OK by finding security in codes, rules, and laws. This is the pride of self-righteousness and the area where conscience often operates — conscience not as a life guide but as a way of self-justification by which we defend, vindicate, and right ourselves.

This is the danger of pharisaism against which St. Paul warned. The problem of the keeper of the Law is not that he doesn't keep it well enough, but that he thinks he is justified by his keeping of it. That is why St. Paul speaks of the Law's increasing sin. The Law increases sin because the more we keep it, the more we think we are justified or OKed by our actions. And when we fall short of our self-imposed standards, we are filled with guilt.

Third, the threat of not-OKness to our Child results in rebellion against the threat. Our Child tries to get out from under the "oughtness" that hangs over his existence by denying its validity. The result is that we lower our standards or throw them all away.

Pride acknowledges the threat of not-OKness and seeks self-OKing, which becomes illusory self-righteousness. Despair acknowledges the absolute inevitability and inescapability of threat. It takes threat with absolute seriousness and, if unresolved, can result in suicide. Rebellion denies the validity of threat and the possibility of being

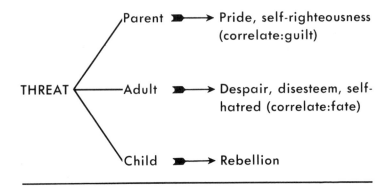

```
                   Parent  ▶──→  Pride, self-righteousness
                  /               (correlate:guilt)
                 /
                /
THREAT ◀───────── Adult   ▶──→  Despair, disesteem, self-
                \                 hatred (correlate:fate)
                 \
                  \
                   Child   ▶──→  Rebellion
```

questioned. It moves out of the questioned stances of pride
and despair and becomes the questioner before whom
rules, others, and even God must vindicate themselves. Its
results are destructive of self and society.

Life under threat

Do these people sound familiar?

PRIDE: "Nobody can criticize me! I'm not
like those hypocrites in that church.
I follow the Golden Rule!"

DESPAIR: "It's hopeless. I can't do anything
right. I wish I were dead."

REBELLION: "Don't tell me what to do! I'll do
what I want when I want. Rules
were made to be broken."

On the other hand, the Gospel is the ultimate, unconditional affirmation of God acted out in Jesus of Nazareth,
whom we trust in spite of and instead of threat. The Gospel
does not remove threat nor destroy the identity of the ego
(old Adam), but rather confers a new identity (new Adam or
new man) which exists in tension with the old. It calls for

tance, (2) confession, (3) forgiveness, or absolu-
(4) repayment or penance. Consider the story of
ncounter with Zaccheaus (Luke 19:1 ff).

us comes to the house of Zaccheaus, a notorious
ctor, has table-fellowship with this man with whom
ould not associate, and whatever was said, when
aus comes out again he is a changed man. *He gets
mind" about himself*. It is apparent that he has per-
Jesus to be the Friend of sinners, as his Affirmer.
e result is surprising and startling. Zaccheaus is
give up his trust in money and his exploitation
ple. Jesus' comment on it all is that on this day sal-
has come to the house. Zaccheaus has repented; he
nfessed his wrongdoing; he has been affirmed and
en and is willing to make reparation to those he has
ited. "I will give half of my belongings to the poor,
I have cheated anyone, I will pay him back four times
uch."

trust in affirmation instead of trust in threat, for denial of self-affirmation, for trust in Jesus as the Affirmation of God.

The nature of the self

What are the dynamics of the self under the Gospel? How do the Parent, Adult, and Child in us function?

If the Gospel operates in the Parent, it becomes Law. The self-justification cycle begins anew. Only this time one is not justified by correct behavior but by correct believing. The Gospel becomes information about either what to believe or what to do.

If the Gospel is received by the Child, it becomes justification for license. Since God is forgiving, it doesn't matter what is done. If it is man's nature to sin and God's nature to overlook it, then the world is seemingly well arranged.

It becomes clear that for the Gospel to remain Gospel, it must live in the Adult, where it confers a new identity on the total self.

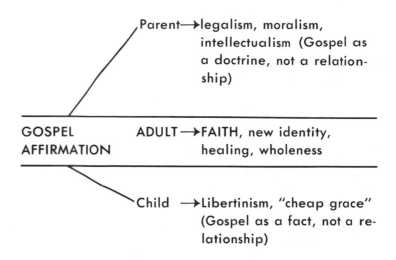

Parent→legalism, moralism, intellectualism (Gospel as a doctrine, not a relationship)

GOSPEL AFFIRMATION

ADULT→FAITH, new identity, healing, wholeness

Child →Libertinism, "cheap grace" (Gospel as a fact, not a relationship)

The "precariousness" of the Gospel now becomes evident. For only if the Gospel operates in the Adult in the face of threat will it be perceived by the self as Gospel.

At the same time, the Gospel does confer a new identity on the Adult, and in the decision-making process enables servanthood through the shifting of values. In a similar way, Christianity, which is the Gospel in the world, offers society a new identity and mediates between civilization and nature. In the political sphere it offers a third alternative between revolution and repression and is thus the true humanizing force in the world, which it evaluates and transforms.

That the Gospel also works in the world is significant for you because there is both an individual and a social dimension to your identity—your self-understanding and your relationships.

Each of us has his own unique self-understanding. But this is shaped by our relationships with others. For example, John Doe is the son of Fred Doe. He is the husband of Myrna Doe and the father of Dottie and Donna Doe. John is a brain surgeon, a member of Mount Calvary Lutheran Church, and belongs to the AMA. These relationships confer on him a social identity and a position and place in time, space, and history that influences and forms his personal identity, what he thinks of himself.

A faith or unfaith relationship to the absolute threat and affirmation of our God also confers, forms, and influences identity. The Christian faith makes a new self-understanding possible and opens up new possibilities for our other relationships. For Jesus is God affirming us in a way that neither exploits, indulges, nor manipulates as often happens with the affirmations we give each other.

Neither does He enslave us as do the affirmations of

our gods, whom we must
He gives us our new iden
destructive guilt over our
giveness without despair ove
anxiety toward the future a
cues us from the boredom of
the "respondability" to be tr
is around us. He allows us to
with love. He frees us from t
and provides us with a new
gives us freely through our ne
that He is our new relationship
of reality.

When people encounter Jes
as Gospel, they are called to tru
rather than threat. They unders
way, get a "new mind" about th
by seeing themselves as affirm
reality. This makes possible a new
healing of relationships. Identity
static. It is a descriptive rather tha

Instead of defining what this
confers is, some of the things that it
described:

1. We acquire a new awarene
   about reality, truth, and ourse
2. We accept responsibility for ou
3. We accept forgiveness, tru
   rather than threat.
4. We discover the possibility of
   we restructure our value syste
   servanthood.

Theologians describe our new iden

(1) repe
tion, an
Jesus' e
Jes
tax coll
most w
Zacche
a "new
ceived
Th
able t
of pec
vation
has c
forgiv
explc
and
as m

8.

CHRISTIAN,
YOU'RE A NEW MAN!

The new self in action

Repentance/ confession/forgiveness/repayment is one dynamic process. The component factors are ultimately inseparable. As we saw in the last chapter, Zaccheaus' repentance and receiving of forgiveness immediately and automatically resulted in reparation, because trusting in Jesus (faith) resulted in a shifting of his values. So also with us. Servanthood is not the result of faith in the sense that it is an entirely separable or optional thing. Rather, servanthood occurs in the very act of faith and the changing of the object of our trust, which brings about immediate value shifts.

In this sense the meaning of the troubling passage "faith without works is dead" becomes clear. The very act of faith, itself, changes behavior. These four (repentance/ confession/forgiveness/servanthood) go together. Confession without receiving forgiveness can be merely pride: "Look at me, I admit my mistakes!" Forgiveness without confession confirms illusory self-righteousness: "God loves me. So what else is new?" Works without faith can be self-justifying and hollow: "Look at all the good I've done!" Repentance without forgiveness is despair: "Look how rotten I am!" It appears that any of these four without the whole process can become the religious game of unfaith. Religious games are the most demonic because they occur where we think we are most right and righteous. When the struggle of the Christian faith is lost, when we feel most secure, then the danger of Christianity becoming a religious "game people play" becomes greatest.

Our new identity results in new possibilities for the Adult's relating to Parent and Child. Under threat the Adult perceives itself as caught between the competing, often contradictory demands of the judgmental Critical Parent and the self-centered Rebellious Child.

Under affirmation the new self can shift to a more productive evaluation and use of the positive aspects of the Nurturing Parent (concerned with care and preservation) and the joyful and spontaneous Creative Child (who adds much of the joy, happiness, and sparkle to life). This part of the Child will be unashamed to do the joyful, natural, and spontaneous things that our Critical Parent makes the Adult repress most of the time. Putting flowers in our hair. Walking in the rain in puddles with our shoes off. Being natural and open with others.

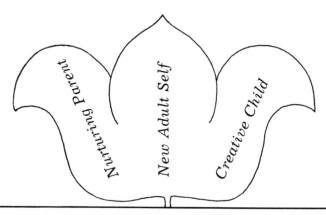

Nurturing Parent
New Adult Self
Creative Child

Eight-year-old Marion Mackles shows how the Child in each of us can daily recreate the the world, washing it with the fresh words of our imaginations.[22]

I saw a fancy dancy dress
hanging on a fancy dancy window
of red roses you could call it a red
rose window I put it on and I
danced to a swan of bees I put
it on a chair of rock and I looked
at the sky of hand I put on
my fancy dancy dress I fell
asleep and I had a dream
of blue sky of roses and a
house of daisies

and I awoke and it was true
I saw everything I saw
sky of roses house of daisies a tree
of orange a book of apple and
I loved it all and I lived with it for
the rest of my life

[22] *Wishes, Lies, and Dreams.* Reprinted by permission of Random House, Inc.

But there is a battle going on within us as we shift our trust from threat to affirmation. The new self does not replace the old but they live in tension.

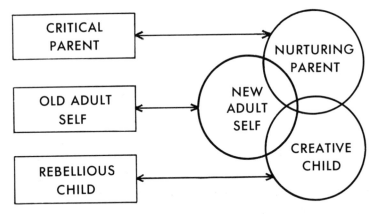

Our old self-understanding sees itself caught in guilt because it does not live up to the demands of the Critical Parent, the Adult's despair, or the Rebellious Child's throwing away of any standards. Our old self-understanding tries to defend itself from these threats and figure out how it can vindicate itself in the face of the overwhelming demands of the Parent and the false freedom of the Child.

Our new self-understanding sees itself as forgiven, as able to live under judgment and with guilt without despair.

It can appropriate the energies of the Child without its self-centeredness and destructive irresponsibility. It can tap new forces in the Nurturing Parent and the Creative Child for a new level of peaceful, joyful, and responsible living. The Christian is freed from his Critical Parent and Rebellious Child and is freed for the happiness of the Creative Child and the servanthood of the concerned Nurturing Parent.

But this new self-understanding results from a shift in trust that is not a once-for-all-time occurrence. It does not replace the old, but lives in constant tension with it. So there is the need for constant renewal — constant giving up of the old, letting go of self-justification and inappropriate defensive responses. The threatened, destructive self must constantly die. And we need continuing affirmation from the Gospel and the forgiving love that resurrects our new selves from our ashes of despair and mistrust, anger, fear, and guilt.

For this reason we view repentance, confession, forgiveness, and servanthood as a continuing process not a one-shot event, as a life-style in which we Christians engage. The new identity conferred on us by God's redeeming verdict makes this new life-style possible.

The baptismal life-style

This new life-style, which we can call a **baptismal life-style**, is the life-style of the church. It is a baptismal life-style because through baptism the Christian community involves us in the life of repentance and forgiveness. Baptism is our initiation into God's promised life-style. The old self dies (confession and repentance), and the new self rises to new life (a new life created in faith, conferred in forgiveness).

Jesus ties his own baptism closely to His death. He says to James and John: "Can you drink the cup I must drink? Can you be baptized in the way I must be baptized?" (Mark 10:38). Or, "Will you share My life-style? Will you be baptized by My death and thus also share My resurrection?" The baptismal life-style is expressed by Jesus, "If any man would follow Me [live My new life-style], let him deny himself [give up his old, self-vindicating self], take up the cross [die to the old self and sin—a painful business!] and follow Me [simply trust My affirmation]."

And the Christian life-style is based on the possibility of newness of life. St. Paul tells us that the Christian baptismal life-style is not to get a person ready for death, but it is for life—a full, new life! "For surely you know this: when we were baptized into union with Christ Jesus, we were baptized into union with his death . . . *so we might live a new life.*" (Romans 6:3-4)

> i thank You God for most this amazing
> day: for the leaping greenly spirits of trees
> and a blue true dream of sky; and for everything
> which is natural which is infinite which is yes
>
> (i who have died am alive again today,
> and this is the sun's birthday; this is the birth
> day of life and of love and wings; and of the gay
> great happening illimitably earth)
> how should tasting touching hearing seeing
> breathing any—lifted from the no
> of all nothing—human merely being
> doubt unimaginable You?
>
> (now the ears of my ears awake and
> now the eyes of my eyes are opened)
>
> —e. e. cummings[23]

The new Christian life-style is found in the church. The church is all of us gathered together in the name of Jesus (in faith in the Gospel), encouraging each other in our new life-style of repentance and faith. The Christian community is all of us believers gathered around the Word of God, living out a baptismal life-style, and celebrating our faith in hearty table fellowship. We are a community

[23] Copyright 1950 by E. E. Cummings. Reprinted from his volume *Complete Poems* 1913—1962 by permission of Harcourt Brace Jovanovich, Inc.

of Gospel believers — Gospel that is proclaimed in our midst as Word and celebrated as Sacrament. That is the church — all of us together living under the Word of God.

Because the Word of God (how we experience God now) is threat (judgment) and affirmation (grace), when it is so proclaimed we can say of our community with Mark: "The kingdom of God is at hand. Repent *and* believe the Gospel." Our community is a repenting and believing community, trusting in Jesus as the Gospel.

The kind of activity we as Christian community experience can be summarized:

threat and judgment	*affirmation, love, forgiveness*
not-OK	OKness conferred in faith
God's NO	God's YES
death	new life
repentance	belief in Jesus as the Gospel
crucifixion	resurrection
self-justification	receiving God's justification
sinner	saint
outcast	son of God
old self	new self

(or in psychological categories)

uptight	freed-up
defensive	open
hostile	reconciled
threatened	affirmed
self-deception	self-actualization

We experience both threat and affirmation simultaneously. The Christian community is not static. It is those of us who are engaged in the struggle between faith and unfaith, trusting our own gospels and trusting Jesus as the Gospel, feeling ourselves to be not-OK, or self-OKed, and accepting God's promise, His OK verdict.

Each of us must be given an opportunity for confession and repentance in an atmosphere where we know that such confession will not be used as a weapon against us. (Here the church has much to learn from the kind of mutual acceptance that goes on in many sensitivity groups and which allows for such open confession.) The opportunity for confession and for the experience of the affirmation of the Gospel must be given in an individual, personal way.

This is not an individual faith ("me and You Lord") but a community faith in which we all share as each of us becomes personally involved in the community struggle. Our self-justifications, bad faith, and false gospels need to be exposed in a loving, trust-encouraging way, and we must be given the Gospel in which to believe. We must be such a community to one another.

This means that we must know and be concerned with our brothers, with their struggles and turmoil. Then we can support and uphold one another in the Gospel. The church is like a chain of mountain climbers, all roped together in faith, ready to pull and support one of the group who may be falling.

We must be concerned with whether we are living out a baptismal life-style, are really engaged in the struggle or have capitulated to our old self-understanding, with its pride, despair, and rebellion.

Our goal is not to indulge, encourage, or OK one another in illusory false gospels but to make genuine repentance and faith possible. The experience of threat and retribution is everywhere present. In a Christian community living out the affirmation of God, sewed to one another in mutual word and action, that affirmation can also become a real, concrete, and vital force in our lives.

Example I: value-negating behavior

If the Christian community is going to use TA, it should not give up its own unique understanding of self-justification, values, and the search for affirmation. We must not forget whose we are. But we can also learn how we are from modern psychology. For example, the computer-like speed and fashion with which we make our value choices is truly remarkable.

Consider this illustration. Doctor X was telling his good friend Y about what he considered to be incompetence on the part of another doctor. Y then asked who this other doctor was. Since X valued the affirmation of Y's friendship more than his professional obligation to remain silent, he immediately, almost without thinking, behaved in an unethical fashion. As a doctor he has an obligation to report his knowledge to no one but the appropriate examining board. But instead, he instantly replied, "I shouldn't tell you this, but since you ask, it's Dr. Z!"

Let's analyze this statement in three parts:
1. I shouldn't tell you this (awareness of value),
2. but since *you* ask (justification for negating value),
3. it's Dr. Z (value negation).

Transactional Analysis can tell us that this transaction probably has two ulterior motives or components. First, there is a Parental critical-judgmental aspect in the condemning of the other doctor ("the joy of gossip"). Second, there is a Child rebellion against an external authority, in this case the medical code of ethics.

Christian analysis adds a *theological* motive behind

these psychological motives: (1) Parental judgment—"I'm a better doctor than this incompetent idiot!" This is self-justification, making myself OK, building myself up at the expense of another by tearing him down to show that I am better. (2) Child rebellion—"Standards, medical ethics, they don't apply to *me!*" This is the self-justifying denial of authority which is expressed in the total irresponsibility of the negation and in the flaunting of a reasonable and preservative code of ethics. "I know I shouldn't tell, *but* I'll do it anyway!"

Now, if X had been aware of the dynamics of self-justification and the possibility of God's affirmation in trust in Jesus, he could have broken the old cycle of pride (Parental superiority based on the judgment that "I'm better than the other guy") and rebellion (the Child's "I'm above standards of ethical conduct that apply to others"). While X properly values Y's affirmation and what he thinks of him, he should have seen it in the proper perspective of God's higher affirmation. "God affirms me. I need not negate my ethical values to keep my friend's affirmation."

X then could have said, "I can't tell you because it would go against the ethics I've pledged to uphold." This would be a positive value affirmation. Further, "In fact this whole conversation is really improper because it's unfair gossip [confession], and I shouldn't judge others except in the proper forum [acceptance of responsibility]."

What would result from this? The cycle of retribution would be broken, for Y would understand why he was not told—not because he wasn't trusted, but because of the doctor's own trustworthiness. Y does not need to respond in hurt or anger—"All right don't tell me. See if I care!" Rather he is free to respond positively—"Yes, I can understand that."

104

Value negations occur constantly "in the little things" of life. But it is possible to change our life-style if we become aware of what we are doing and why.

Example II: a redeemed transaction

Psychologists describe neurotic behavior as a behavioral response out of proportion to the stimulus.

If a husband asks his wife out of mild curiosity and not in an accusatory tone where she has been, and she responds with an angry temper tantrum, he may well be hurt, shocked, and surprised and wonder what is going on.

Or, a wife asks her husband if there's gas in the car since she has to leave early in the morning. He, feeling guilty over deliberately leaving it almost empty because he was too lazy to stop and fill it on the way home, responds in an outburst, accusing her of being responsible since she drives it more than he does. It is clear that the dynamics of guilt and self-justification are operating here as he tries to preserve his rightness and innocence. The nonthreatened person can say something like, "I'm sorry I didn't fill it, I was too tired to stop."

This is a good illustration of why the Christian must add the dynamics of threat and self-justification to his use of Transactional Analysis. First, the husband perceives the wife's Adult statement as threatening. Since he feels guilty, he interprets a clearly fact-finding Adult question as a Parental condemnation—"Why the hell didn't you fill the tank, you idiot!"

This would be true unless this is what Transactional Analysts call an ulterior transaction, in which the real message is hidden or disguised under an acceptable Adult message. The hidden message would probably be tipped off by facial expression or tone of voice.

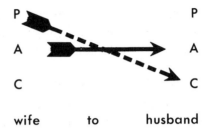

wife   to   husband

The straight line is the verbalization; the dotted line represents the ulterior message, perhaps something like, "You're just my big baby who can't do anything right, can you!?"

Let's assume it's a straight forward Adult-Adult transaction. The husband can express any of his three ego-states: (The Adult is given two possibilities.)

> P — "You use the car more than I do and it's up to you to keep it full."
>
> A-1 — "I'm sorry, I was too lazy to stop and fill it last night."
>
> A-2 — "I'm sorry, I forgot!
>
> C — "That's your problem."

Responses P and C are theologically self-justifying attempts to avoid responsibility and to establish innocence in the face of perceived threat. If the husband used either of these and was familiar with TA, he would realize that his Parent or Child has responded. He could then defuse the pending fight by saying, "I'm sorry; you hooked my Child," or "my Parent." If he had caught himself beforehand and moved to the Adult state, giving response A-1, he would be making the appropriate, honest response. But he could also have used A-2, another illusory protestation of innocence, as were P and C.

How would his Christian nature help him here? Sensitized to self-justification and God's justification, he would not need to feel threatened. God affirms him specifically, e. g., at 9 o'clock, in the living room, in front of his wife Gladys. Our man doesn't have to create his own OKness by attempting to prove his rightness and innocence to his wife. Nor in our little daily dramas do we.

If he has used P or C, immediate and active repentance is available: "Boy, I'm sorry. I'm really being defensive. I should have got gas."

If he used A-2, faith frees him to say: "I'm sorry. That wasn't true. I was just too tired and lazy to get it."

His Christian wife also could help. After P or C she could stop the "cycle of retribution" with "Honey, you don't have to be so uptight. God affirms you. You're OK. I forgive you."

The Christian Gospel of God's affirmation really frees us, absolutely, from the illusions and defensiveness that alienate us from others. We don't just give "positive strokes" any more, like petting a cat. We give the love of God to each other in our love. We don't affirm others to exploit them — manipulating them for our own ends: "I better be nice to the old lady tonight; I got bowling tomorrow and the Cardinals on Saturday."

We Christians express our love and faith in concrete ways — everyday, everywhere. Our living faith is a beautiful and positive force in our lives that permits us to see ourselves and others honestly, openly, and truly. In our faith community we accept each other as we are, without indulgence, for we know we are affirmed and dare show ourselves to our world.

Really, we are beautiful. It sure is a wonderful day.

Here are some exercises in Christian living. If you have others, pass them on to your friends.

1. Write a "praise God" or "thank God" song, poem, or statement of your own, one that you feel intensely. Don't make it about abstract things. Make it about the world you live in and the events that are your life. Let the words you have inside you rush out. Don't worry about mentally editing them. Then say your praise, or sing it, to God.

2. Write your confession. You may want to write it for one, two, or several voices. Then make an appointment with your pastor and take it to him. Explain to him its origin; then read it to him or let him participate in it. And talk with him.

3. If you are married or have a close friend, sit with that person where you are quiet and alone. If you feel like it, hold his or her hand. Then speak a confession and absolution to each other. Tell your partner the good news of salvation for both of you. Then let him confess to you. Then speak to him the forgiveness Christ has retrieved for both of you. Now reverse the process.

Close with the words "I love you; God has made us right with each other. We are friends."

4. Gather your children or friends. Then each of you say a part of a prayer for each of you. If there are three of you, you would say a part of three prayers—one prayer for each person participating. Encourage your children to pray whatever they would like to pray for their brothers, sisters, and for you. You do the same. If what they say is funny and they laugh, feel free to enjoy your prayers with them. After all, you all really are OK.

9.
IT'S UP TO YOU

"It's up to you" summarizes the main thrust of this book. Nobody else can take responsibility for you, your life, and your actions. It's up to you. Fritz Perls said that whatever we look to for affirmation becomes in reality our judge. Do you want to be judged by threat or "judged" by the love of Jesus? You must make the choice to live out a threatened, defensive, hostile life or an affirmed, liberated, open life.

This final chapter is a summary, study guide, and workbook. It's a chance for you to see what you have learned and whether you can put that learning into practice — first in the following exercises and then in your life.

This book has focused on a few key concepts which examine and explain aspects of your life, your actions, and reactions. These are threat and illusion, threat and idolatry, and threat and self-justification. These form a structure, or cycle, of retribution under which we all live. It is here that we experience not-OKness, the need to feel OK, and the drive to create OKness at any cost.

Do you understand these dynamics? Are you now sensitive to and critical of their operation in yourself and others?

The Gospel of God's forgiveness offers us affirmation that breaks our bondage to this enslaving cycle of hurting others as we have been hurt. It opens us up to the possibility of loving as we have been loved. We have talked a great deal about new life, new identity, and new action. Now it's up to you!

Take out several sheets of paper so you can write down your answers. If you are studying this book as a group, obtain copies of the songs and poems ahead of time. You may still want to write down some of your thoughts before discussing them.

I

Listen to and carefully read the Simon and Garfunkel lyric "Flowers Never Bend in the Rainfall." The song's chorus begins, "So I'll continue to continue to pretend." Why not sing along?

Then answer the following questions:

1. What is the general feeling of the song? Joy? Sorrow? Despair? Hopelessness? When have you felt the same way? Why?

2. What does the song say about illusions? About reality? About death?

3. What is the root cause of our illusions? What does illusion have to do with God, threat, and idolatry?

4. What does the song say about God, truth, and right? And about how we experience them?

5. What is the dilemma the song poses? How does the song resolve it? How would you after reading this book?

6. What are your own pet illusions? Do you think you're better than others, never wrong, don't need anybody?

7. Why are your illusions so important to you? Why do you defend them? How can you deal with them?

Having trouble? Look at chapters 2 and 3 again.

II

Read Robert Frost's poem "The Road Not Taken," which begins "Two roads diverged in a yellow wood." Then answer the following questions:

1. Does the speaker feel that he made the wrong choice in taking the road "less traveled by"? How do you know from what he says in the poem? What, then, does he regret?

2. Why does the choice between two roads that seem very much alike make such a big difference to him later? What are the roads symbols of?

3. Why do choices among things we value make us feel guilty? Do we have the choice, then, not to choose?

4. What is TA's answer to value negation and guilt?

5. What is the answer of the Christian faith?

Refer back to chapters 5 and 6 if you need some help.

III

Two songs by Paul Simon present two very different attitudes toward life. One is "Patterns," which contains the thematic line, "Like a rat in a maze the path before me lies." The other is "Bridge Over Troubled Water," which gives the comforting words of one who helps in times of trouble.

Listen carefully to both lyrics and pay special attention to the music, which is also significant.

Then answer the following questions:

1. These two songs present two alternatives. What are they?

111

2. Does the first song say you are responsible for your life? Why or why not?

3. Is your life fated and beyond your control? If so, why do you *feel* responsible for it? What answer does the song give to that problem? Is submission to fate redemptive? Or is it threatening?

4. What attitude toward life does the second song express? Does it express a way of living with others? Do you think it describes a Christian life-style?

5. Can you imagine Jesus saying those words to you? How does that make you feel?

6. Compare that feeling with the way the first song makes you feel. Which way would you rather feel? Do you have the choice?

For further help look again at chapters 7 and 8.

Now choose the song that fits the following words:
A. "Patterns"   B. "Bridge Over Troubled Water"

1. threat   _____   _____

2. responsibility   _____   _____

3. freedom from   _____   _____

4. lack of
   responsibility   _____   _____

5. affirmation   _____   _____

6. freedom for   _____   _____

Answers: A, B, A, A, B, B

112

IV

The following true story depicts a rather typical event — getting a ticket. But can you see what's going on beneath the surface?

John drove to the library. He parked beneath a sign that said "NO PARKING, 4–6 p. m." It was 4:30. He knew the sign was there, but on this occasion he had forgotten it. When he came out, his car had been towed away. John walked to the police station and was very angry. The stupid police had no right to tow *his* car away.

He said, "I want my car back," and threw the $15 at the policeman behind the desk. Officer Jones picked it up, got red in the face, and threw it back at John. "I don't have to take that. Now you try it again," he said. John handed the money back, got his receipt, and walked out silently. Later at home he felt unhappy and uneasy.

Analyze this story using TA and the theology we have discussed in this book. Write down your ideas. What is really going on here? What could John have done differently? What could he have done after he had gone home?

If you have trouble with this section, reread chapters 7 and 8, especially pp. 103–108.

When you have finished, compare your analysis to the one following. (Or, if you're in a group, first discuss your analyses with each other.) How did you do? Try doing the same kind of thing with an event from your life. The goal is to become aware of what you are really doing and saying, and to be able to change your actions while they are happening.

Analysis: John has made a simple and natural mistake. He has forgotten the no-parking zone. Instead of admitting his mistake, he blames the police. His Child has been hooked. It is their fault not his. This is his whining Child: "Why do people do things like that to *me!*" TA takes us this far very well. It would say he should have kept his Adult in control. But why can't he admit his mistake? TA tells us: because he feels not-OK.

But why can't he take responsibility for his action. Our theological analysis tells us he feels threatened and his not-OK burden requires him to justify his actions, himself, and indeed his whole life! This self-justification results in his passing along the hurt. He creates an illusion of innocence in order to put the blame on others. It is not his fault. It's the stupid police! Stretching all reason and logic, he feels at this moment that the rules don't apply to him.

The next step: If it's *their* fault, make them pay! So he is sullen and hostile to Officer Jones, who in turn passes the hurt right back. He's had enough for one day! His Child is hooked, overruling his moderate Adult, who could understand how John felt coming out of the library and finding his car gone, and he strikes back. He expresses his Child by throwing the money back and resorts to his Parental authority as a policeman. "Now you try it again." The implied threat is: "Or I'll throw the book at you."

By now both are caught up in the cycle of retribution, and the only alternative is for John to leave in anger, with his hurting Child, and officer Jones to express his self-satisfied, Critical Parent: "I guess I showed him!" At home John feels guilty but is not consciously aware of it. After all, he was right, wasn't he?

V

The following prayers express the concerns of this book. They seek to relate prayer to experience so that daily life in all its aspects can be related to faith. Read them aloud. Write some prayers of your own that express areas of concern in your life. Can you then live those prayers? Make prayer a life-style rather than the mumbling of meaningless words. Prayer changes things if you let what you believe shape your life and actions.

Strangers

I met a man I never knew;
I still don't know him.

I rode an elevator with another.
We paused and went our ways,
never acknowledging that one
another existed.

I rode a bus, eyes front,
eyes out a window.
Never face to face,
eye to eye,
with my brother.

O God, touch me, heal me,
show them to me
as more than names
and nameless faces.
Not just a mob, but persons
with wants and needs and cares.

Perhaps then I could ease one

Sunday Football

What a great way to spend a day!
The thrill and excitement of football,
the perfect combination—
skill speed, power, and coordination.

Funny thing about football though:

You only win at the expense of others,
usually by intimidating, humiliating,
and DESTROYING them.

That's not like the Gospel kingdom, where
a new order is created
and a new way of dealing with others.

Lord, it's a new ball game.

The Shower

The American soap industry is floating on
a great bubble of success.
America should be the most godly nation in history,
if godliness is next to cleanliness.

But it's not, and we're not, and I'm not.
Or perhaps cleanliness of spirit is meant.
But even the soap industry cannot touch
the depth of me.

I may try other means to clean me up:
money, power, success,
liquor, drugs, sex, or psychiatry.
But TA is not God,
and neither are these others.

I trust in you, Jesus.
You can clean off the layers
of alienation, hate, and fear
that separate me from You and others.

Morning Prayer

Good God! Good day!

The rising sun,
The risen Son.

Both remind me of
the possibilities
for newness.

A new day, a new life,
lived in Your light.

VI

You are now ready to answer the questions raised by
the title of this book, *Who Says I'm OK?* Below are some
of the more popular answers:

1. The American Dream
2. Marxism
3. The quest for the ultimate orgasm
4. Wealth
5. Social standing
6. Drugs
7. "My country right or wrong"
8. The Christian faith
9. Eastern mysticism
10. Family
11. Power
12. "Dropping out"
13. Transactional Analysis
14. The scientific method
15. Deterministic psychology
16. Racial superiority
17. Progress
18. Education
19. Work
20. Astrology

Choose wisely. It's up to you!

APPENDIX

"Yes and No in a Taxicab," by Walter R. Bouman, from *The Cresset* (January 1971). Reprinted by permission.

This dialogue took place approximately as described. Imagine a clergyman getting into a taxicab. The driver throws the first words over his shoulder in the direction of the clerical collar he glimpsed when the clergyman got into the cab.

Driver: Where to?

Clergyman: Airport, please.

D: You a priest or something?

C: I'm a Lutheran pastor.

D: That so? I used to go to a Lutheran Church. St. Paul's on the north side. Pastor X baptized my kids. Know him?

C: Yes, I do.

D: Yeah? I liked him a lot, but I don't go much any more (Pause) You know, I got a theory about religion. *All religions are OK if you practice them.*

C: (Not interested) That so?

D: Yeah! Every religion is good so long as you put it into practice.

C: (Suddenly deciding to take the conversation seriously) Could I test your theory?

D: Sure, go ahead. Always like to talk about religion.

C: What would you say about Hitler and Nazism? Was that a good religion?

D: (Surprised) That wasn't no religion!

C: But it had many of the characteristics of a religion — rituals, doctrines, heretics. Most important, Hitler demanded and got total loyalty and unquestioning obedience. The institutions of Nazism replaced those of Christianity almost item by item. What does that do to your theory that every religion is good so long as you put it into practice?

D: Well, you sure got a crazy definition of religion!

1. C: How so?

D: Well, I always think of religion as, well, you know, churches and praying and preaching and that stuff.

C: And if you don't go to church you're not very religious?

D: Well, you know, like I said, I sorta got away from it.

C: Maybe you did. Or maybe you just got away from a churchly kind of religion. And maybe religion could include a lot more than church. For example, what are you loyal to? What do you care about?

D: Lots of things — like bowling. I sure like to bowl, twice a week. Pretty good average, too. 169. You bowl?

C: A little. But is bowling the most important thing in the world for you? Does it have your highest loyalty? Would you do *anything* to bowl?

D: No, guess not. It's not important like that.

C: What is?

D: I guess — well, my kids, maybe. They're pretty important. Even got me to got to church for a while — you know, St. Paul's. That's how much I'd do for them! One's in college now. That's why I drive a cab a couple a nights a week — and weekends. I need the money for the kids — though I got a good enough regular job — at Mac-Donald, right out where we're going.

C: You'd do anything for your kids?

D: I guess so. Anything. My boy — the one in college, you know — studying engineering — he'll be drafted when he's done. Another year. Way it looks, he'll probably go to Viet Nam. I think I'd go for him if I could. I was in the last war, you know. Germany.

119

C: That so?

D: Yeah. Guess I'd do anything. Wife says I care too much. But what else a man got to live for. No, take my kids away and I don't care anymore.

C: Sounds like that's your religion.

D: I thought you were gonna say that. I sorta knew what you were driving at way back when you asked what I cared about. Tried to change the subject cause I know what you're gonna say. You're gonna say I worship my kids — just like the wife says.

2. C: Well do you?

D: Aw right. Lemme tell you. Yeah! I do. And it bothers me. I used to go into their rooms at night when they were little — and they'd be sleeping — and I'd love them so much I could just feel it. And I knew I couldn't stand to have them suffer, and when they were sick it was worse on me than it was on them. I knew if one of 'em died it would be awful. I knew I couldn't stand it. I would even pray once in a while, that God wouldn't let 'em die. I thought going to church might help. But then there didn't really seem to be a God. 'Scuse me, Reverend. I don't mean to insult you.

C: That's OK. Go ahead.

D: Finally it just seemed useless, all that singing and praying and sitting and standing. Mind you, I'm not against religion. Good for the kids to get some starch into their lives, something to keep 'em straight.

But I knew that if something was going to happen to 'em, it would. Nothing I could do. So what the hell — 'scuse me, Reverend. You got me going here. I went to church often enough to please 'em till I got this weekend taxi job. They knew I was working for them. Keep 'em safe. Keep 'em straight. Give 'em a good education. That's all I can do. Till they get drafted and get sent to Viet Nam. And get shot to hell. And me with 'em. I know that's the way it will be. And I don't know what to do. What do I do? And don't tell me to believe in God. That

120

don't work. I tried.

C: I'm not going to talk to you about God; but we can talk about religion because you *have* a religion, and you're practicing it right now. Driving this cab. You don't have to believe there *is* a God because you already have a god: your kids. I could say even more. You use your kids to justify your life. That's what keeps you working and living.

D: Well, what's wrong with that?

C: Why don't you tell me?

D: Oh, hell! Don't play games with me.

C: I'm not; really I'm not. I think you already told me what's wrong.

4. D: When?

C: When you talked about how you loved your kids and ended up thinking of one of them dead, maybe in a war, and you not able to do anything about it.

D: I still don't get it.

C: Look, the point you yourself are making is that you have a god, something that says YES to you, something that justifies your existence. Everybody who goes on living has made or found that kind of YES for life. That's why Camus . . .

D: Who?

C: Camus, Albert Camus.

D: Never heard of him.

C: That's all right. The point is, he said that suicide was the only important philosophical problem. If we go on living, it's because we have a god, a YES, something that affirms us.

The thing you are beginning to realize is that your YES isn't all that dependable. You can't count on your kids being what you've asked them to be: your "god." That's the trouble with all our religions, all our "gods," all our causes and affirmations. They are not God. They are not able to be what we make them. We have to work

121

overtime to pump "life" into our "gods." That's what enslaves us, finally. Our home-made gods always demand more than they can deliver.

D: But my kids are good to me. Couldn't ask for more.

C: Sure they are. But they can't be the whole ball of wax. And they won't be either. It's not just Viet Nam. They grow up, marry, move away from home. They need us less and less.

D: Yeah, that's happening already.

C: Besides, none of us ever succeeds in justifying our lives — even if our "gods" outlast us. Death says a final NO to everyone of us.

D: Wait a minute! I don't look at death like that. It's just, when your number is up, you've bought it.

C: I'm not talking about how we look at death; I'm talking about the fact of death. Some people are saying that "God is dead." It may really be that death is God, that death is the inescapable verdict upon each of us.

D: You make it sound like I'm guilty of something. But 5. I don't feel guilty. Nothing wrong with loving your kids.

C: Right — not if that's all you're doing. But if loving them is the way you justify what you are and what you do, then you are already living an evaluated life. And then death, too, is an evaluation. It says NO.

D: That's pretty hard to take. I didn't ask to be born. I didn't ask to be made this way.

C: That's part of my point. When we can't justify ourselves, we can always try to blame something, or someone, or the system itself. Anything to make sure that we are never in the wrong.

D: Say, aren't you preachers supposed to comfort people? None of this sounds very comforting.

C: Well, we started talking about religion, remember? Trying to test your theory that all religions are good as long as you practice them. I've tried to say that we all have a religion, a way of getting a YES for life, a way of not being in the wrong. And it seems to me that our religions really fail us, that we are betrayed by our religions into deceiving ourselves and blaming others. The verdict on that kind of living is death.

D: But you didn't say anything about God.

C: You said you didn't want to be told about God. So we talked about life and failure and the verdict of death. That may be all the glimpse we get of God from life and history. And the God we see there is not some grandfatherly being who makes everything come out all right in the end. You yourself said that there didn't seem to be that kind of God anyway. The only God we're likely to meet if we look for one in life and history is the God that says NO to life and history.

6. D: But aren't you supposed to tell us a way out?

C: I don't think so. Whatever else I might have to say, it's not a way out. Christianity is not some cheap escape from the way things are. You can invent an escape if you want, but it won't take you anywhere. You can even try to make the Christian Gospel into some kind of escape, but that's as much an invented religion as any other — and just as much a failure.

7. D: Well, what is Jesus supposed to do?

C: He doesn't let us off. He lets us *in* on Himself, on what He is and on what He does. He is YES to us, and HE asks us to believe that and to give up our other "gods" and justifications. His best known stories were about Himself, because He was accused of saying YES to people who didn't have much going for them socially or morally or religiously — whores and traitors. He told about a son who took his inheritance and left home . . .

D: Yeah, yeah, I know. "Prodigal son." Right?

C: The point of the story is that Jesus is a different way of dealing with rejected people. We might call it "forgiveness," but it does not come cheap. Jesus' death is His final and total commitment to us. It is the way He experiences the verdict, lets it happen to Him, our homemade religions and our illusory justifications.

The boy in Jesus' story gets that kind of YES which sets him free to admit that he is in the wrong. We are given that YES in Jesus which sets us free to say NO to our religions, even to join in the verdict upon them because the YES is stronger than the verdict, because when the verdict has done its worst, the YES overcomes it.

D: I never heard it that way before.

C: But that's what Christians mean by "Gospel." To believe that Gospel means to entrust ourselves to the YES in Jesus, to hold to that YES against the NO of life in history. To believe Jesus is to be free for all the things in the world out of which we want to make gods—for bowling and kids and work and the wife. We are really free *for* them because we don't need any longer to try to make them what they can't be: our gods. We're not trapped into working them up into something divine. We're free to be *for* them as Jesus is *for* us.

8. D: Well, where does church and praying fit into all this?

C: It helps if we stop thinking first that church is a building or a religious organization. Church is really what happens to people when the Gospel is happening to them and through them to other people. The words that Christians share with one another about Jesus as God the Forgiver are meant to set them free for one another and for all men.

D: Doesn't sound like any church I know.

C: Maybe we all have to ask where this is really going on. It's true that a lot of religious action going on under the name of church is only a cover-up for our old home-made religions. A German play written right after World War II is about a man who comes back from the war and finds himself betrayed by everything. The church is a character called "god" in the play, who keeps repeating, "Nobody cares about me anymore." That's what a lot of "churches" ask for—that people care about them. But the author shouts, "Hasn't God studied theology? Who is supposed to care about whom?"

124

When the church cares about itself and worries about whether people care about it, then that's a sure sign that the Gospel is being missed somewhere. The Gospel sets people free from wondering who cares about them, sets them free for caring.

9. D: You mean even church religions aren't all right when you practice them?

   C: I'm saying that churches and doctrines and even the Bible can be misused so that they become "gods" and false gospels. Right religion is where Jesus' affirmation is being heard and trusted and celebrated so that men are free for each other. Wrong religion is not trusting the Gospel that is in Jesus — and that kind of religion can be going on in the middle of churches.

10. D: Does praying do any good?

    C: Like everything else, that depends on whether praying grows out of trusting the Good News in Jesus. When you believe the Good News, you can hold your whole life and the people in it; your world and its destiny, before God. Praying then means getting to be a "son of God" like Jesus, that is, knowing and trusting and saying thanks for the YES that sets you free. Then you will recognize God's YES elsewhere in the world, and you will look for ways to be part of the YES in the world. . . . This the airport?
    D: Yeah.

11. C: Here. Keep the change.

    D: Thanks.